PUZZLE QUIZ AND STUNT FUN

JEROME S. MEYER'S

Puzzle

Quiz and Stunt Fun

SECOND REVISED EDITION

DOVER PUBLICATIONS, INC., NEW YORK

Published in Canada by General Publishing Company, Ltd., 30 Lesmill Road, Don Mills, Toronto, Ontario.
Published in the United Kingdom by Constable and Company, Ltd., 10 Orange Street, London WC 2.

Puzzle Quiz and Stunt Fun, first published by Dover Publications, Inc., in 1956, is a new selection of material which originally appeared in Jerome Meyer's *Fun-To-Do,* published by E. P. Dutton and Company, Inc., in 1948 and in *Puzzle Paradise,* published by Crown Publishing Company in 1945.
The second Dover edition, first published in 1972, incorporates extensive corrections and revisions.

International Standard Book Number: 0-486-20337-9

Manufactured in the United States of America
Dover Publications, Inc.
180 Varick Street
New York, N.Y. 10014

TO

EDITH BROWN

CONTENTS

PREFACE

"Entertainment" is a big word with thirteen letters in it. If it is treated carefully it will work wonders; if abused, it will turn sour and produce first-rate boredom. This is just as true of a book as it is of a movie or television program.

This book is primarily a book of entertainment. It is *not* a collection of clever, difficult puzzles that requires a knowledge of differential calculus, nor is it the 11,836th book of questions and answers, otherwise known as "another quiz book." In writing this book I have tried to eliminate all those warmed-over gags that were so popular in the Gay Nineties—enigmas like the man who can't marry his widow's sister and the big Indian who isn't the father of the little Indian—and to produce many new items. In other words I have tried to make this book just as original and new as an entertainment book can possibly be.

In the "This 'n That" section you will find nearly one hundred miscellaneous things which are neither quizzes nor tests. Some are unbelievable statements which are unique and interesting; some are tongue twisters for reading aloud; some are entertaining things to do and might be used for games; while others are just pure stunts like dipping your bare finger into a glass of water without wetting the finger or drawing a perfect circle composed entirely of long, perfectly straight lines. In a great many cases it is pure guesswork with a big surprise awaiting you on the answer page. An example of this is the question of how large an ordinary housefly would be if it were enlarged in size one billion times (it would be larger than the moon). It is difficult to describe just what is in this section—you will have to browse through it and see for yourself. It is really an ice-breaking introduction to the new and entirely original quizzes and word puzzles that follow.

If you hope to find crosswords or double crostics or word squares in the word-puzzle section you are in for a disappointment. Nearly all of the word puzzles included here are *basically* new in design. With the exception of one or two DUO-TESTS which have appeared in a magazine, these word puzzles have never appeared anywhere. This is also true of the TRIPLE-WORD puzzles which have never been published in any magazine, newspaper or book. These original creations have their beginning here and, in sending them out into the big wide world, I sincerely hope they will be fun to do.

Now, the quizzes are something else again. A quiz, you will say, is a quiz no matter how thin you cut it. It must have questions and supply answers, otherwise it is not a quiz. That is true, but there are any number of ways of presenting quizzes. The idea, for example, of calling for the greatest number of *wrong* answers in a quiz which is extremely difficult to answer wrong, is surely a new wrinkle for any quizzard to iron out. Then there are a number of crazy quizzes with riddle-like answers as well as a few mix-you-up quizzes, quiz games and loads of others entirely different from the cut-and-dried, run-of-the-mill, question-and-answer variety. A special section on vocabulary quizzes is included for those who pride themselves on their choice of English as well as for those who would like to increase their vocabulary and have fun at the same time.

For the convenience of the reader all problems, quizzes and puzzles have been numbered consecutively with corresponding numbers in the answers in the last section of this book.

In conclusion, I want to thank *Coronet* magazine for permission to reprint many of my quizzes and short items which ran in their Game Book section as well as *Reader's Scope* magazine for permission to use some of my vocabulary tests from their

Fun with Words section. Acknowledgment and thanks are also due Gerald L. Kaufman for the four word puzzles: Weighted Words, Automotive Words, Sextuple Anagram and No Duplicates.

J. S. M.

THIS 'N THAT

1. A FEW NEAT TRICKS

CAN YOU FIGURE THEM OUT?

a. How can you stick paper or playing cards on a smooth wall without the use of any kind of glue, paste, adhesives, tacks, nails or any other solid or liquid?

b. How can you pick a dime off a table and drop it into a glass on another table without touching the dime or table with any part of your body or without using a knife or any metal, cardboard or wooden instrument to lift it?

c. How is it possible to place two oblong mirrors in front of you in such a way that you can read in them the type on this page normally?

d. Joe and Fred had lunch together. When the dessert came Joe took a lump of sugar and set it on fire but when Fred tried to do it the sugar would not burn. What did Joe do to the sugar to make it burn?

2. THE REMARKABLE EGG

Williams had a handsome peacock who laid an egg in Simpson's automobile while it was parked on Robinson's farm. Since this egg was valuable all men claimed it. Williams said it was his because his peacock laid it. Simpson claimed it because it was found in his car. Robinson said it was his because it was found on his farm. The matter of ownership was taken before an eminent judge who threw the case out of court. Why did his honor do such a seemingly rash thing?

3. HOW TO STAND AN EGG ON ONE END

It is said that Columbus was the only man to stand an egg on one end. That may have been true in the fifteenth century but with our modern eggs you can do it fairly easily. Just shake the egg thoroughly for a few minutes and this will break the yolk. Now allow the broken yolk to settle, and stand the egg on a table with a cloth on it. The egg will stand if you do the balancing carefully, but be sure that there is a cloth on the table.

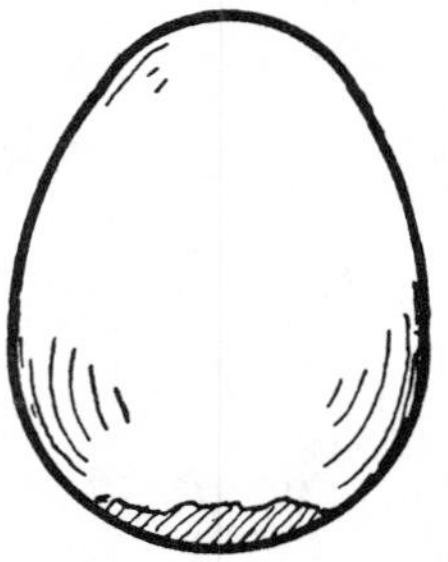

4. IT'S AGAINST ALL LAWS OF PHYSICS

Who says that no two bodies can occupy the same space at the same time? You can do this little experiment and disprove this universal law. Just fill a glass to the brim with water and drop one pin after another into it. You will find that you can drop at least two hundred pins into the glass without displacing any of the water or, in other words, causing the water to overflow. You can do the same with one-inch brads.

5. IF YOU DON'T KNOW, GUESS!

Guess High:

a. If an ordinary housefly were enlarged in size one billion times, how big would that housefly be?

Guess Low:

b. If a steel band were stretched tight around the earth at the equator so that it touched that imaginary line everywhere, how much would the band increase in length if it were raised one foot above the earth's surface?

Guess High:

c. If the national debt from World War II were paid in pennies, placed next to one another in a single line, how long would that line be? (That debt was more than $250,000,000,000.)

Guess High:

d. If it were possible to put one grain of sand on the first square of a checkerboard, two grains on the next, four on the next and so on, doubling the quantity each time, how much sand do you think you would have by the time you got to the last square?

(*See next page*)

6. HOW GOOD ARE YOU IN PHYSICS?

a. On the previous page is a wire cage with a canary inside. The cage weighs four pounds and the bird weighs three ounces. If the bird rests on the rungs of the cage, the bird and cage together will undoubtedly weigh four pounds and three ounces which is the combined weight of the bird and the cage. But suppose the bird flies around inside the cage, how much will they both weigh then? Will the bird's weight vanish in spite of the fact that he is inside the cage, or will both bird and cage still weigh four pounds and three ounces?

This illustration shows a little monkey on a string which goes around a pulley and has a weight on the other end of it. The weight and the monkey are exactly the same—they just balance each other—so if the monkey remains still nothing happens. But suppose the little fellow starts to climb the rope, will the weight go up or down on the other side?

7. WHAT ARE THESE TWO THINGS?

What is it that is neither animal, vegetable or mineral? It is neither solid, liquid or gas. It is a definite thing that we all see every day and it multiplies itself although it is not alive. It is never still and is extremely important to us all, for it would be almost impossible to live without it. It is not part of any person or any thing yet it could be part of everything. Can you name this mysterious thing that is so important to us and that we all see every day?

What is it that you can touch but cannot feel? That you cannot live without, though it is totally useless to you? It moves and is clearly visible under certain conditions. It changes color constantly and can fall on anything without smashing. You were born with it and are continually losing the darn thing but you really don't care because you know that it is sure to return to you. The average person gets rid of his when he goes to bed although some have it in bed too. Can you name this mysterious something that is so important to us and that we see almost every day?

8. A FEW "QUEERIES"

Of course you will say, "I don't believe it!" to these few "queeries," but all you need do to be convinced is to turn to the answer page and read the explanations. Here we go:

a. If it were possible to cut a large sheet of thin paper in half, and cut that half in half (making quarters), and cut those quarters in half (making eighths), and so on for fifty-two times, and then stack all the pieces, the pile would be more than 150,000,000 miles high!

b. Rio de Janeiro in South America is nearer to a point in Greenland than it is to a point in Mexico!

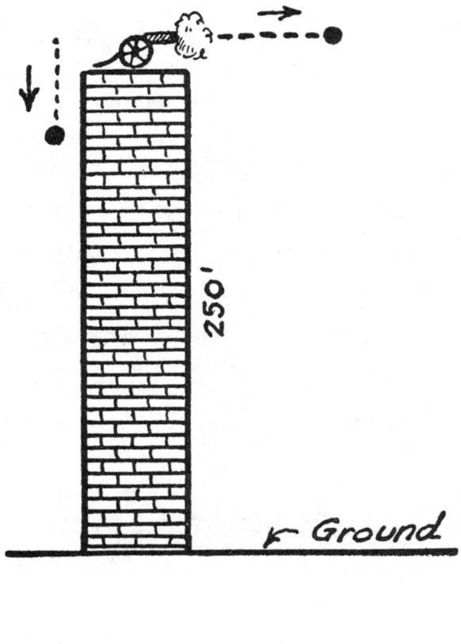

c. Two cannon balls, identical in size and weight, are taken to the top of a tower 250 feet high. The first ball is shot horizontally from a cannon the very instant that the second ball is dropped. The first ball travels four miles while the second ball drops only 250 feet, yet they both hit the ground at the same time!

d. Water can be made to boil until it actually freezes!

e. Two airplanes, identical in size and wing spread, fly over a field on a sunny day. The first plane is 500 feet above the field and the other plane is only 50 feet above the field. In spite of this the shadows of the two planes are the same size—there is no measurable difference in their shadows.

9. MUCH ADO ABOUT NOTHING

My little nephew shot this poser at me the other day: "If I add nothing to a number it remains unchanged, if I take nothing from a number it remains unchanged. Now, if I multiply that number by nothing I don't multiply it by anything at all, and I say it should remain unchanged. My teacher, however, says that if any number is multipled by zero the result is zero. Who is right and why?"

Can you supply a sensible answer to this?

10. A LEGAL GEM

Three attorneys had lunch together in a New York restaurant, A treating B and C. They all ordered oysters and B, not caring for so many, gave one of his to C saying, "I know you like to eat oysters more than I do." C removed the oyster B gave him and found a beautiful pearl in the shell. "Thanks," he said to B, "for this valuable gem." Now B, being a capable lawyer, argued as follows: "I gave you the oyster to eat and you have done so. The shell is mine for it is a means of conveying the oyster to you, just as my china plate would convey fried eggs to you in my home. The shell was given to me by the waiter and is still mine." At this point A piped up with: "I invited you fellows to eat with me and I am paying for the meal. Everything that you don't eat is therefore mine, since I am paying for it. Unless C eats the shell, that shell belongs to me." Of course C claimed that the pearl belonged to him since B gave it to him. Now the attorney for the restaurant owner, hearing all the commotion, came over and said: "Sorry, gentlemen, all these oyster shells belong to my client who is under contract to sell them to a road-making firm. He is in the food business and not the jewelry business and if a gem is discovered in one of his oyster shells it is his good fortune."

To whom does the pearl belong?

11. WE PUT YOU ON THE SPACHT

Ivor Izweckschski was learning English slowly. He finally became resigned to the *ough* dilemma and succeeded in pronouncing thr*ough,* en*ough* and th*ought* all correctly. One day he handed a friend the following word (if you can call it that) and told him to pronounce it according to our rules of English. Can *you* pronounce PHOTI?

12. THE $103 QUESTION

A man bought a watch for $103 including the tax. Being a rather unusual fellow he paid for it in eight bills, but they were not five twenties and three ones as you might think. They were eight other bills and there were no one-dollar bills among them. How is this possible?

13. GENTLE HINT

The daughter of a friend of mine had a suitor whom she did not like. One evening when he was visiting her she became so bored that she put down nine circles on a piece of paper thus:

O O O O O O O O O

and asked the young man if he had ever heard about the nine O's. When he said No she added five vertical lines to the circles and he took the hint. What did she do?

14. THE ABSENT-MINDED PROFESSOR

Every day old Professor Radcliff commuted from Lynbrook to New York. Each morning he would get to the Lynbrook station and climb aboard the first train that came along regardless of the direction in which it was going. Obviously he boarded the wrong train frequently but not as often as you might imagine. It so happened that every ten minutes a train *from* New York pulled into the station and every ten minutes a train *to* New York arrived at the station, both trains pulling out almost immediately, but the two trains going in opposite directions never arrived at the same time. So here we have a picture of a train arriving at and leaving Lynbrook station on its way to New York, every ten minutes, and another train arriving and pulling out of Lynbrook station on its way to Babylon, every ten minutes, and yet these two trains are never in the station at the same time. Here we also have the old professor getting to the Lynbrook station every morning and taking the first train that comes along. Wouldn't you think that he would be taken out of his way fifty percent of the time? The fact is that he gets to New York *eight times out of every ten!* Can you figure out how this happens?

15. DRY WATER

Have you ever seen dry water? You can actually put your bare finger in it without getting the finger wet. It is all very simple. Just fill a glass with water and add a teaspoonful or two of zinc stearate, letting it float on the surface of the water. Now, if you put your finger into the water for not more than an inch you will find that it is perfectly dry when you take it out in spite of the fact that it has actually been in the water. Try it and see for yourself.

16. FIFTEEN MATCHES

Arrange fifteen matches in a row on a table and take turns with a friend removing one, two or three of them at a time. The object is to make your opponent take the last match. You can always do this if you see that either 13, 9 or 5 matches remain on the table when it is your opponent's turn. Obviously if he starts by taking 3 matches it is too late to leave 13 on the table, so you will have to figure on leaving 9 and, consequently, you also take 3. Now, no matter whether he takes 1, 2, or 3 matches you can always arrange it so that there will be five matches remaining and force him to take the last match.

17. PIGS AND PENS

Is it possible to put nine pigs in four pens so that there is an uneven number of pigs in each of the four pens? Try to do this with pencil and paper.

18. ODD MAN OUT

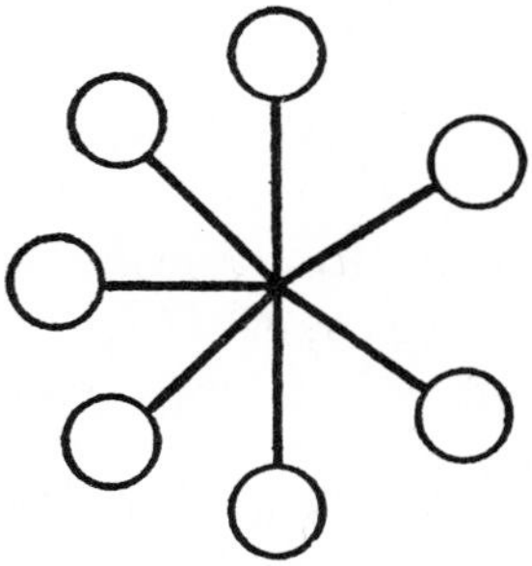

In this diagram start with any circle, count 1, 2, 3 and put a dot in the third circle. Keep doing this, starting with any other circle, except the circles that have dots in them, and try to fill all the circles except one with dots. You should have six circles with dots in them when you have finished. This is not easy to do.

19. A HOT ONE

It burns no coal or any other kind of fuel and it is not connected in any way with an electric current. It is not on fire and there are no flames touching it yet it is hotter than all the stoves and furnaces in New York City when they are heated to capacity. What is it?

20. CRAZY READING

The following unpunctuated passages are tongue twisters and brain teasers. First see how fast you can read them aloud, then reread them with the expression of an elocution student. Finally, explain the situations described without laughing or even smiling. You won't find this so easy to do.

a. Why Went Went Without Go

Mr. Go and Mr. Went had a date to see a ball game so . . . Go knew Went wanted to go but it depended upon when Went went so Go went to Went to get Went to go but Went told Go to go so Go went After Go went Went went after Go to tell Go to go not knowing Go went to phone Went not to go When Went went to tell Go to go and when Go went to let Went know Go wanted Went not to go is not known and that's why Go went without Went and Went went without Go.

b. See, Sore and a Seesaw

Mr. See and Mr. Sore were old friends. See owned a saw and Sore a seesaw Now See's saw sawed Sore's seesaw before Sore saw See which made Sore sore with See Had Sore seen See's saw before See's saw sawed Sore's seesaw then See's saw would not have sawed Sore's seesaw But See saw Sore and Sore's seesaw before Sore saw See's saw so you see how See's saw could saw Sore's seesaw It was a shame to see See see Sore so sore with See just because See's saw sawed Sore's seesaw.

c. A Tough Fight at the Fort

General Fite stormed the fort of General Fort Fite fought at Fort's fort before Fort could fight Fite but Fite's unfortified fort enabled Fort to fight Fite better than Fite fought Fort So Fite fought Fort and Fort fought Fite at Fort's fort and Boy how Fort fought Fite If Fort had fought Fite before Fite's unfortified fort instead of Fort fighting Fite before Fort's fort then Fort and Fite might not have fought and there would be no need for Fort's fort and Fite's fight.

21. SIMPLE MATCHIC

Place a cigarette on a clothless table. Now take a wooden match and rub it on your coat sleeve several times, explaining to your friends that this will generate static electricity in the match. Now do the same with the cigarette and be sure to tell everyone that both match and cigarette now contain the same kind of static electricity and they will therefore repel each other. Now place the cigarette on the table and bring the "electrified match" near it. The cigarette will slowly be repelled and the effect is terrific! Of course the secret is quite simple. All you do when you bring the match near the cigarette is bend over it enough to blow *very gently* on the cigarette without being observed. Make sure that you blow *gently* because the cigarette has to move away *slowly* and not quickly.

22. YOU WON'T BELIEVE IT UNTIL YOU TRY IT!

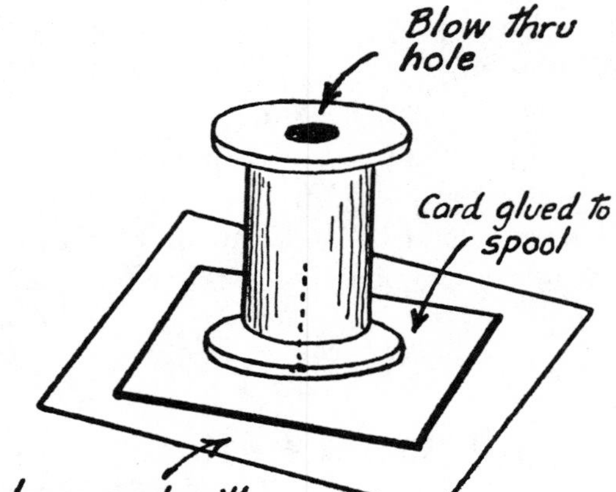

A thin piece of cardboard is glued to the bottom of an ordinary spool and a hole put in the card so that you can blow through the spool. Now another card (a playing card) is held against this, as shown, and a pin penetrates this card and projects up into the hole in the spool. If you take your hand away of course the card will fall. Oddly enough, if you *blow* on the spool, and blow hard, the card will be held tightly against the spool and will not fall off! This certainly seems hard to believe! Just try it and see for yourself. Hold the card with the pin in it against the glued card and blow on the spool at the other end. The loose card will *not* fall or be blown away.

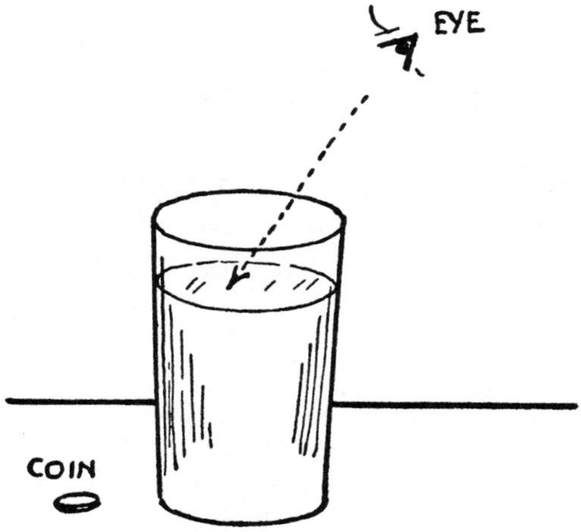

Who says that good clear drinking water is transparent? Just fill a glass with water and place a coin behind it as shown here. Now look at the coin through the top of the glass, viewing it through the surface of the water and through the other side of the glass. If you can see it you're truly remarkable!

23. CELLEMENTARY, WATSON!

A prisoner on a ship traveling from Argentina to New York was kept in his cell three decks below the main deck during the entire voyage. In his cell was a washbasin with running water, an army cot and a small ventilator in the ceiling. Not knowing anything about navigation and not being able to go out on deck, how was the prisoner able to tell when the ship had crossed the equator and was in the Northern Hemisphere?

24. COME 9, COME 18

Here is something that seems very peculiar: no matter what number you select between 10 and 1000, your answer will always be either 9 or 18 if you do the following:

First: Add the digits in the number and subtract the result from the number itself.

Second: Add the digits in the new number.

Here is an example: 865 is a number picked at random. Add the digits and you get 19. Take this from 865 and you get 846. Add these digits and your result is 18. It always works.

25. DO YOU SPEAK ENGLISH?

Here is a little tale that a Londoner told a woman from Marshalltown, Iowa. The woman had always thought that she spoke English but after hearing this story she decided that maybe she didn't. Do you feel the same way or can you figure out what this gentleman was talking about. There are 22 expressions that are different in our two languages. How many can you "translate"?

There was something the matter with our lorry the other day. After working over her for about a fortnight I lifted her bonnet and found that her accumulator was out of order. This necessitated my buying a new spanner at the ironmongery. It cost me two bob. Just at this point my braces broke, which embarrassed me because my vest kept showing. I suggested to my wife that we visit the nearest bazaar where she could purchase some bags. She said that was a fine idea because she also needed some nibs, two wireless valves, a radiator and a good torch, while I ought to get myself a new boater. After shopping we asked a navvy to direct us to the nearest snack-bar where we could get some good bubble and squeak and warm scones. On the way home my wife expressed a desire to go to the cinema, but I said I preferred to sit in the stalls of a good variety as there were too many queue-ups at the cinemas.

26. THE CLEVELAND BUTCHER

Meat prices were so high last October that a Cleveland butcher was ashamed to post them in his window. Instead of this he put up the following sign and offered to give C pork chops to anyone who could solve the problem, which is simple division. He explained that each letter in these two words is a number and C is greater than 2. You can see that PORK divided by CHOP is equal to C which is a number greater than 2. Here is the sign the butcher put in his window:

$$\frac{\text{PORK}}{\text{CHOP}} = \text{C}$$

It is up to you to solve this by using logic and common sense. There is only one answer which can be easily checked and you don't need any knowledge of mathematics to do this. All you need are good sound powers of reasoning and a little common sense. What numbers of four digits do PORK and CHOP represent?

27. THE FACE IS FAMILIAR

Most people know that Washington's portrait is on the one-dollar bill and Lincoln's is on some other bill, but they are not sure which. What about the other bills? Whose portrait is on the $1000 bill or the $5000? If you are willing to do a little work you can find out for yourself, without looking at the answer, the portraits on all of the bills. Here is the information and it is up to you to figure it out:

Madison, Grant and Cleveland together make $6050.
Franklin, Jackson and Lincoln together make $125.
McKinley, Jefferson and Jackson together make $522.
Chase and Madison together make $15,000.
Franklin, Washington and Grant together make $151.
Hamilton's portrait is on the $10 bill.

Name the correct portrait on each bill from $1 to $10,000.

28. THE MARK OF EVIL

The mark shown in the box below is the mark of evil. It is the symbol of murder and terror. Millions have died for it and millions have died because of it. Can you tell what it is?

29. ITS IMPORTANCE CAN'T BE EXAGGERATED!

This is the diagram of something that saved our important cities from destruction during World War II. It was by all odds the most important thing in the war and its importance today can't be exaggerated. What is it?

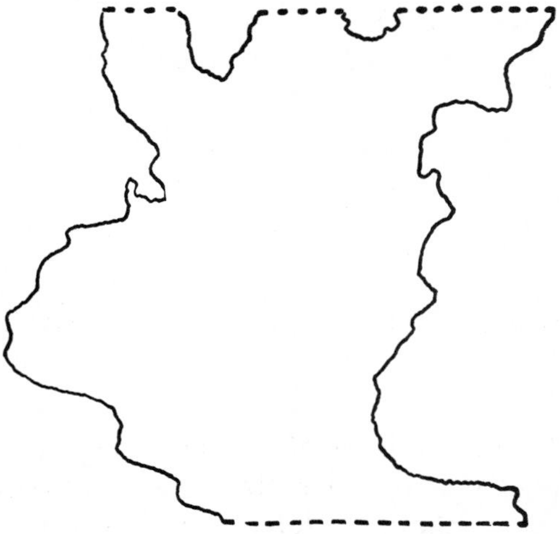

30. THE INNOCENT LETTER

During World War II the following apparently innocent letter was found on a suspicious character in London. Scotland Yard examined the letter carefully and found that it was mailed from New York and contained a message of great importance to the enemy. Can you decipher this message?

Dear Hans:

I just bought a house by the SEA and OH how you would ENVY me if you could see it. I have asked you to visit me many times and now I say OH WHY don't you come?

I have just completed a long ESSAY on a man who was made EYELESS in this war. His old mother died recently at EIGHTY.

Come to visit me OH ANY time next week—maybe FRIDAY.

Yours
Fritz

31. ARE YOU WORTH YOUR SALT?

Spill a little salt on a bare table, then try to remove it without touching the salt with anything, without blowing it, or fanning it or touching the table. How can you possibly do this? If you give it up, see answer section at end of book.

32 IT HAPPENED ON THE GRAND JURY

Jones & Co. were stockbrokers. One of their customers, a Mr. Blank, bought a number of stocks from them and wanted a receipt. Finding the office staff too busy, Mr.

Jones himself told Mr. Blank to write out the list of stocks on his stationery and he would check it over and sign it. This Mr. Blank did, itemizing the stocks in his own handwriting, and Jones signed the receipt. Blank then folded the receipt and put it in his pocket. Six months later Blank returned to Jones & Co. and demanded his stocks, but when Jones saw the receipt he realized that $25,000 worth of stocks had been added. Of course an argument followed and Mr. Blank brought suit against Jones & Co. for grand larceny. But the D. A. was able to prove beyond the shadow of a doubt that it was a case of forgery on the part of Mr. Blank and the grand jury indicted Blank. Now, the question is: How was it possible for the D. A. to prove beyond doubt that the $25,000 worth of stocks was added to the receipt *after* Jones had signed it. Remember, the listings were in Blank's handwriting and there was plenty of room between the last listing and the signature to insert other items.

33. THAT MYSTERIOUS NUMBER

If I add 1000 to a certain whole number the result is actually *more* than if I multiplied that number by 1000. What is the number?

34. SEVEN ARCS AND WHAT THEY DO

Most people are so sophisticated these days that all they have to do to get what they want is to make seven arcs of circles with one finger, and in many cases they only make a single arc to be heard anywhere in this world. What do these people do?

35. THE MOUNTAIN LAKE

The little town of Junkville needed to find approximately how many gallons of water there were in a near-by lake. Now it was well known that no water entered this lake or left it and the amount of water that evaporated from it was negligible. Engineers set out to find the lake's area and test its bottom for depth, but the mathematics involved in this procedure are not accurate enough since there was far too much variation. This threw the little town of Junkville into a dilemma until a bright young chemist appeared and solved the problem. Can you possibly figure out how that bright young man found the approximate volume of the lake?

36. HOW COME?

Jack and Jill were born on the same day of the same year and are the children of the same parents, yet they are not twins. How come?

37. FIVE STRIKES, YOU'RE OUT

What is a five-letter word meaning "to strike a blow" and which has the following properties: you can make, from the five letters in that word, five other words, each beginning with a different letter included in that original five-letter word? Assuming that you get that word, the new word will commence with the second letter of that word and will contain all its letters, the next new word will begin with the third letter of the original word and have all the same letters in it, and so on. What is the word and what are the four other words that can be made out of it?

38. I DON'T BELIEVE IT

Did you know that you can hold a glass filled with water, and covered with a thin piece of cardboard, upside down, and no water will spill nor will the card be forced off? Try it and see but be sure to fill the glass *full* and experiment over a basin first.

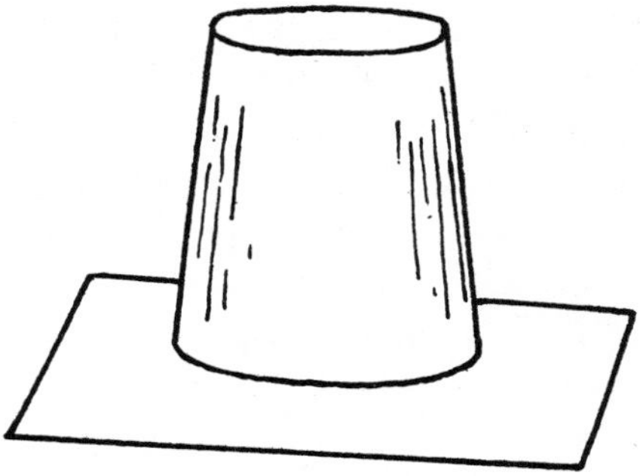

39. THE MYSTERIOUS MAN

He is quoted more than any man in history. His quotations are more numerous than any in Shakespeare or the Bible. Millions look to him for advice and every day read what he has to say in the newspapers, and listen to him on the television and radio. Yet, not one person in a hundred knows his name. Who is he?

40. WHITNEY'S MURDER

The police records of New York City state the following facts in relation to the gruesome murder of Mr. Adolphus Crane. Read this account only once, and remember as much of it as possible. Do not re-read the account before answering the question.

The sergeant at the desk of the ninth precinct received the alarm in the form of a telephone message from Mr. Crane's butler, Whitney, at 2:10 A.M. Whitney pleaded for speedy assistance, saying that he knew who the murderer was. Detectives McCarthy and Blair were immediately dispatched to the house. They arrived at 3 o'clock. At 3:05 the sergeant received another call, which proved to be the detectives. They reported that Whitney had also been murdered. Killed by a shot through the head, he lay in a pool of his own blood. Mr. Crane's death had been caused by a severe beating on the head with a blunt object.

The mystery was never solved. No clues were discovered. The murderer had effectively destroyed the only avenue of approach by killing poor Whitney.

Assuming that the detectives did not kill Whitney themselves, between what specific times must Whitney have been murdered?

41. DOES IT MAKE SENSE?

Millions and millions of Americans are going through pandiculation every day, while other millions are cachinnating and going through phases of sternutation. This condition is enough to make us lachrymose. Do you agree with this and if not why?

42. THE REMARKABLE BROTHERS

The Baldwin brothers are quite remarkable. They both work in New York City. Joe travels more than 30 miles every day without using subways, taxis, buses, trains or anything else that runs on wheels, without flying, passing over water, riding any animal, without walking or running. He passes no streets, no traffic, no trees and no scenery in his daily travels but he is not alone,—he has many who travel with him. Peter, the other Baldwin boy, rides all over the city every day. He is in the thick of the traffic yet he doesn't ride on anything that runs on wheels. How do Joe and Peter accomplish these wonderful things?

43. A HOT AND COLD QUESTION

How can you hold an ordinary paper cup over a gas flame without having the paper cup catch on fire?

44. THE ONLY WORD

There is only one four-letter word in the English language which, when printed in capital letters, reads the same upside down as it does right side up. What is it?

45. COLLEGE, CAMPUS AND COURTSHIP

Andrews, Brown, Casey, Dennis, Evans and Fowler are seniors in one of the following colleges:

Harvard, Dartmouth, Brown, Yale, Princeton and Notre Dame.

I was told that Miss Winters is Brown's girl; Miss Long is Casey's girl; Miss Wilder is Fowler's girl; Miss Skinner is Andrews' girl and Miss Bailey is Dennis' girl.

Now:

Fowler does not go to Harvard. Miss Long doesn't know any Princeton men. Miss Wilder never met any men from Notre Dame. Miss Bailey hates all Dartmouth men. Miss Clark roots for Brown University. Casey knows Miss Bailey but she hates him. Brown wears a big Y on his sweater. Miss Skinner never met a man from Harvard.

To which college does each man go?

46. A REMARKABLE MAGIC SQUARE

This magic square, created by Cipriano Ferraris (Fubine), is certainly remarkable. Not only do all its rows and columns and its two diagonals add up to 34 but there are more than 20 other ways of making 34. Here are just a few:

1	15	4	14
12	6	9	7
13	3	16	2
8	10	5	11

Each small square, regardless of where it is, adds up to 34. Take any square such as 12, 6, 3 and 13 or 15, 4, 9 and 6 or 16, 2, 5 and 11 or 1, 15, 6 and 12—or any other small square and add the four digits and you will always get 34. Note also that the rectangles 15, 4, 5 and 10 and 12, 13, 2 and 7 and also the parallelograms 12, 15, 2 and 5 and 4, 7, 13 and 10 all add up to 34. Of course the four end corner digits 1, 14, 11 and 8 also add up to 34. How many more ways of making 34 can you find?

47. WHEN $4 = 8$

Here is a mathematical proof that $4 = 8$. Just show it to your bank teller and tell him to double your balance.

$16 - 48 + 36 = 64 - 96 + 36$. They both equal $+4$
Then $(4 - 6)^2 = (8 - 6)^2$
or $4 - 6 = 8 - 6$. Hence $4 = 8$. Simple, isn't it?

This is correct algebra but, of course, 4 can never equal 8. Can you tell what is the matter with it?

48. SO BIG THE ARC

Suppose a rail one mile long were laid on the ground and the two ends were pushed together just one foot so that the distance from one end to the other were 5279 feet instead of 5280, how high would the arc be?

49. LOOKING INTO THE FUTURE

A certain year in the future may be found from the following information: If that year is divided by 2, and the result turned upside down and divided by 3, and left right side up and divided by 2, and the digits in the results are turned upside down, the answer is 191. What is that future year?

50. RED HATS AND GREEN HATS

This is by no means a new problem but it is very interesting nevertheless. It is a problem in pure logic and goes as follows:

> Three boys are seated in a room. They all have hats on. A professor tells these boys that he had a total of five hats; two greens and three reds. He said that he discarded two of the hats but did not mention their colors. To test the intelligence of the boys he asked the first boy who knew what color hat he had on to raise his hand. Bill raised his hand right away and announced that he was wearing a *red* hat. How did Bill arrive at this conclusion?

51. IT'S JUST ON THE SURFACE

Can you name a solid that has:

Only one surface?________	Only four surfaces?________
Only two surfaces?________	Only five surfaces?________
Only three surfaces?______	Only six surfaces?________

52. THE SIAMESE NATIONAL ANTHEM

It is said that in Siam they sing the following song to the tune of *America.* Read it over carefully and then have some friend read it aloud and sing it to the tune of *America.* If you don't discover the meaning quickly, then you are just as big an *ass* as he is. The words go:

O Wah Tah Nah SIAM
Gee Wah tan N ah SIAM
Annah SIAM
Yeh SIAM, Yeh SIAM
A Grey begar Siam
Watta grey beg AR SIAM
Annah SIAM

53. THE LARGEST NUMBER

What is the largest number that can be written with three digits? If you say 999 you are far from correct. It is $9^{9^{9}}$ which means 9 multiplied by itself 387,420,489 times. This giant number is so large that if it were written in digits this size it would reach from New York to Kansas City. That number of grains of sand would cover the entire earth to a depth of 10 miles or more. The number of snowflakes that have fallen since the earth began does not even approach this number.

54. TWO PAIRS OF WORDS

By changing one letter in a five-letter word I change its meaning from what women in the Navy are called to what most women are today. What are the two words?

By changing one letter in a four-letter word meaning ocean I get a word meaning dry land. What are these two words?

55. RAILROAD TRIP

In going from New York to Cincinnati, Ohio, on the train, name the states that are entered or passed through.

56. DOUBLE SOMETHING BY CUTTING IT IN HALF

Cut a thin strip of paper about 15 inches long and an inch wide, fold it over on itself and paste the ends together as shown in the diagram. Now take a pair of scissors and start cutting along the middle of the strip (about ½ inch from either edge) and you will think that you are cutting this in two parts lengthwise. But when you have completed the cutting and arrive back at the starting point you will see the paper take the form of a ring twice the size of the first ring. You can also start on the inside surface and end up on the outside by tracing a pencil line along the strip before you cut it.

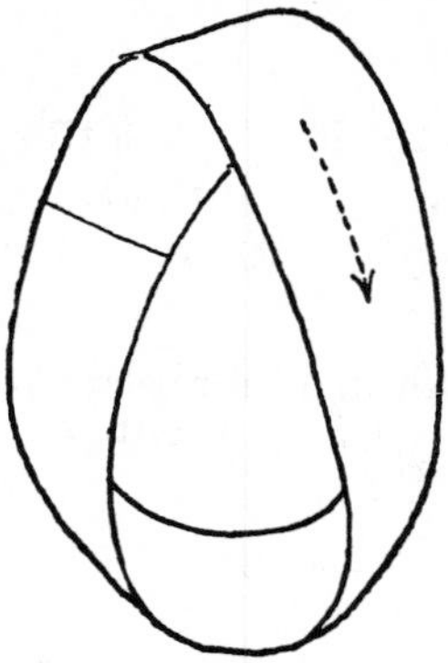

57. MEMORY GAME

This is a lot of fun in small groups and it requires practically no preparation. Just make a list of fifteen or twenty words—any words at all—and number them. Now read the list very slowly to your guests, giving the number first and then the word, but not consecutively. You might read something like this: 6 is coffee, 2 is house, 14 is book, etc. When you have finished the list select one player and ask him to repeat the entire fifteen or twenty words in correct numerical order, starting with 1. This is by no means easy to do and the player who gets most of the words in the right order wins.

58. AS EASY AS PIE

I recently dined with a young couple. We had apple pie for dessert, and knowing my interest in puzzles, my hostess asked me if I could cut the pie into eight equal slices with only three straight cuts of the knife. I gave it up and she did it without hesitation. How did she do it?

59. COLD INDEED

"It certainly was cold in Buffalo yesterday," said Mike. "The thermometer registered exactly zero."

"That's nothing," said Ike. "Where I come from it was just twice as cold as that."

How cold was it where Ike comes from?

60. TEN-WORD SQUARE

Here is a square of 25 boxes. Below the square are 25 letters. Can you fit these letters into the boxes to make five different five-letter words horizontally and five different five-letter words vertically. All words must be different—no two alike. It *can* be done. If you can't make 10 words, make as many as you can and score yourself as follows: five-letter words count 10; four-letter words count 5. Highest possible score is 100. Par is 60.

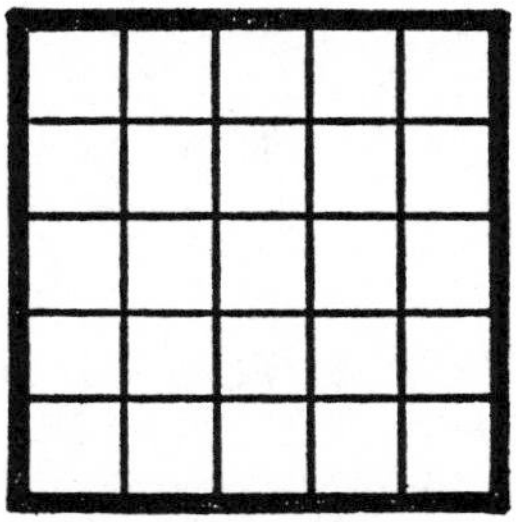

A A A E E E E E E E H L N R R R S S S T T T T V V

61. THE VANISHING BUILDING

In 1946, Mr. A visited and examined a small brick building in New York which he decided to buy. He communicated with Mr. B, the owner, and B agreed to sell. Now A lived in Pittsburgh and seldom visited New York so he made up his mind to wait awhile before consummating the transaction. In 1947, A met a Mr. C who, after seeing the plans and photographs of this building, said he would be anxious to buy it at a price much higher than B wanted for it. A wrote to B and, after a few letters, the deal was closed. A sent the check and B sent A the deed. A now owned the building which he had a right to sell to C. But it so happened that the building department of the City of New York had also examined this building and found it unsafe. They sent B a notice that they had to condemn it but B was in Miami at the time. Of course neither A nor B knew anything about this so when A and C came to New York to look at the building, it had vanished. The building department had torn it down and the only thing A had was a vacant lot. C, angered by the inconvenience, accused A of fraud while A threatened to sue B for damages. B put all the blame on the building department. Can you decide who is responsible for this unusual dilemma?

62. HERE'S A TOUGH ONE

Let us suppose, for the sake of this problem, that the North Pole were habitable. Suppose that by some unknown means of atomic heat it was made into a desirable place to live. Now suppose a small city flourished at the Pole and many other towns and villages also flourished within a hundred miles of the Pole. Call the city at the North Pole, Polis. Since every direction from Polis is south, how would the citizens of Polis describe the direction from Polis of neighboring towns and villages?

63. THE AGE OF REASON

A young mathematician when asked his age replied: "My grandfather was 65 when I was born. Now if you add the square root of the year of the California gold rush (a rational number) to the square root of the year in which a king of England abdicated (a rational number) you'll have Grandpa's age, so all you need do is subtract 65 from this and you'll know how old I am now." How old is this obnoxious lad?

64. A PROBLEM IN REVOLUTIONS

The diagram below shows two wheels bolted to each other on a common center. The little wheel is two feet in di-

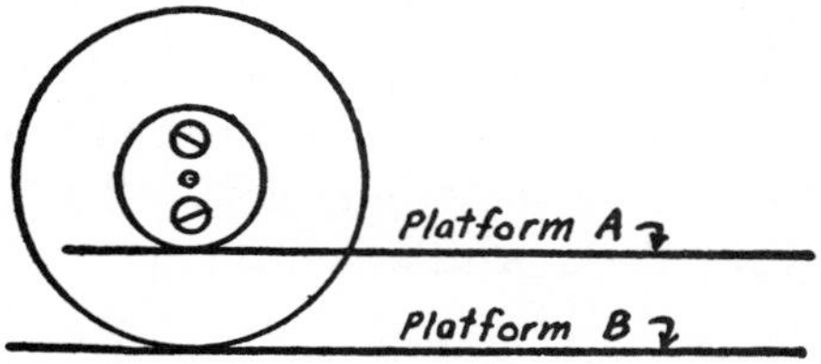

ameter and the large wheel is four feet in diameter. The wheels rotate together, the little wheel rolling along the upper platform A and the big wheel rolling along the lower platform B. Now it is clear that both these wheels make one complete revolution and it is also clear that the big wheel rolls twice as far as the little wheel since its diameter is twice that of the little wheel. But somehow, in a single revolution, they both cover the same ground. How can you explain this?

65. THE STRAIGHT-LINE CIRCLE

Believe it or not, it is possible to draw a reasonably good circle with a ruler and nothing else except paper and pencil. The circle is formed by straight lines about as long as the radius of the circle. Can you figure out how to do it?

66. AND SPEAKING OF CIRCLES

While on the subject of circles how would you go about finding the center of a circle accurately if you just had a ruler and pencil and nothing else? Remember, you don't know where the center is so you cannot get an accurate diameter without doing something first. What is the most practical thing to do in this case?

67. THE PUZZLE OF 30

Can you place the nine even numbers from 2 to 18 inclusive in 9 circles so that any three circles in a line will add up to 30.

68. A NEAT TRICK

With a piece of string, tie a cup by the handle to a doorknob, letting the cup hang down a foot or so from the knob. Now, without touching the cup or string with your fingers, can you cut the string with a pair of scissors without having the cup fall?

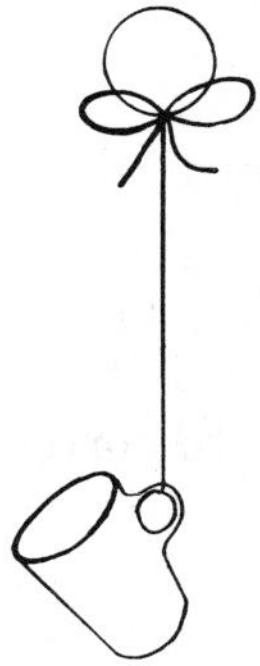

69. WHERE DID THE DOLLAR GO?

This is not a new problem but it is very interesting nevertheless. Three men registered in a hotel and asked for three

separate rooms at $10 each, so the clerk received $30 from the three men. The next day the clerk found that these three rooms could have been let for $25 instead of $30 so he called the page boy and gave him the rebate to give back to the three men. But the boy, not being as honest as he might have been, gave each man back $1 and kept $2 for himself. Now each man, instead of paying $10, paid $9. This makes $27 for the three men since the page boy kept $2. Now 27 + 2 is 29. Where did the other dollar go to?

70. THAT TROUBLESOME HYPHEN

Some of the following words should be hyphenated and some should not. We have purposely made a number of errors in placing the hyphen and it is up to you to locate them and pick out the words that are correctly hyphenated. If you get more than 10 correct you're a whiz.

1. First-class
2. Attorney-general
3. Fellow-citizen
4. Boy-prodigy
5. Four-fifths
6. Anti-American
7. Father-in-law
8. Semi monthly
9. First-aid
10. Lieutenant-governor
11. Sky high
12. Weather-bureau

71. *CHERCHEZ LA FEMME*

These twenty masculine nouns are all looking for their feminine mates. How many of these can you supply? The par for this is 14.

1. Bachelor
2. Executor
3. Author
4. Chairman
5. Deer
6. Maharajah
7. Baron
8. Gander
9. Testator
10. Fiancé
11. Stallion
12. Boar
13. Buck
14. Czar
15. Fox
16. Traitor
17. Drake
18. Jackass
19. Abbot
20. Comedian

72. OVERHEARD IN A PHONE BOOTH

The following conversation was overheard recently. There are twenty glaring errors in English in this short, one-way conversation. How many of these errors can you find? A score of 13 is excellent, 11 is good and 9 is fair.

"Hello Fred. I feel like I ought to call you up to tell you that Edith and me are going to the beach next Sunday. Edith says to me only the other day that she and the children want to go away and between you and I, I think she need the rest because she looks so badly. I told her that she is no different than anyone else.

None of us are able to work through the summer without a vacation. Edith thinks I ought to join her and ask whoever I want to come along. I said it don't make no difference who I ask as long as she is satisfied. I don't know if you would like to come or whether I should ask one of my brother-in-laws, but irregardless of whom accepts, I want you to be the first one invited by Edith and I. Well, old man, let me hear from you as quick as you can because provided you can't come, I'm thinking to ask Peter."

73. THE AMAZING COLOR WHEEL

Believe it or not, the wheel shown here, if rotated on its axis, will actually produce color. If you want to prove this you can either have a photostat made of this wheel and mount it on cardboard and spin it on a pin or you can carefully trace it through a sheet of typewriter paper and blacken it in later and paste it on cardboard. No matter how you do it the wheel, if copied accurately, will show color in the following manner:

When the wheel is spun clockwise the outside ring will be red, the center ring will be greenish and the inside ring will be blue.

When the wheel is spun counterclockwise the outside ring will be blue, the center ring will be greenish and the inside ring will be red.

Don't take our word for it. Get a very good copy of this wheel and mount it on board and spin it. You will see for yourself. You don't need sunlight for this. Ordinary electric light is even better for the purpose. Be sure to use *black* ink.

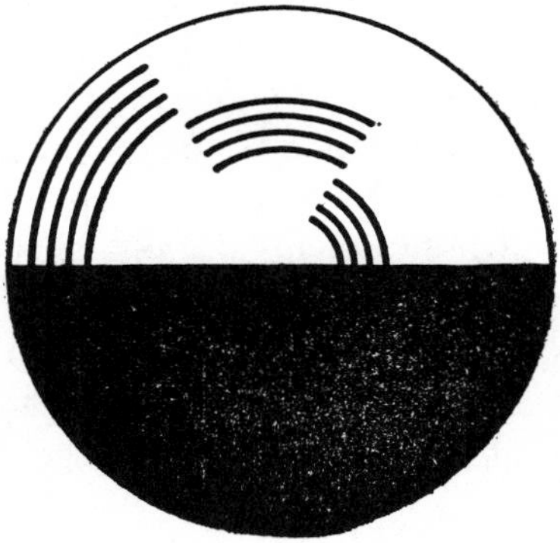

74. MATHEMATICAL WHIZ

If you are willing to memorize a large number—and know it thoroughly—you are in for a lot of fun and can astound your friends with your brilliant mental ability. The number is very easily memorized if you do it in groups of three. Here it is:

5882352941176470

Memorize this as follows: 588, 235, 294, 117, 6470. Say this over and over: 588, 235, 294, 117, 6470. Know it in your sleep so that you'll never forget it and can rattle it off any time, anywhere, like this: 5882352941176470.

After you have memorized this large number write it on a sheet of paper and ask a friend to multiply it by any number from 2 to 12 inclusive. Suppose he says he wants it multiplied by 5. All you do is write down 29411764705882350 as quickly as you sign your name. How does it work? Very simple. This magic number is always *repeating* its digits, and if you examine the last big number you will see the familiar 294, 117, 6470, 588, 235 with a 0 added. Obviously we started at 294 instead of 588 . . . why? In multiplying by 5 we say mentally, "5 times 6 is 30—a little less than 30," and start at 29. You see that the number commences with 588, which is a little less than 600, so no matter what number it is to be multiplied by from 2 to 12, you first multiply by 6 and then find a starting point that is a *little less* than the result. For example:

5882352941176470 × 8 (8 × 6 = 48—start at 47) = 47058823529411760
5882352941176470 × 9 (9 × 6 = 54—start at 52) = 52941176470588230
5882352941176470 × 5 (5 × 6 = 30—start at 29) = 29411764705882350
5882352941176470 × 7 (7 × 6 = 42—start at 41) = 41176470588235290
5882352941176470 × 12 (12 × 6 = 72—start at 70) = 70588235294117640
5882352941176470 × 11 (11 × 6 = 66—start at 64) = 64705882352941170

If you know this number thoroughly you'll be able to do this multiplication mentally and amaze your friends who don't know the secret.

If you have to repeat this just nonchalantly write down the same sequence of digits beginning with 117 instead of 588 and, to all appearances, you have written a new number. Now this "new number" will have the same properties as the original but it starts with 117, which is almost 12, so always multiply by 12 instead of 6 as formerly. For example:

11764705882352940 × 8 (8 × 12 = 96—start at 94) = 9411764705882320
11764705882352940 × 5 (5 × 12 = 60—start with 58) = 58823529411700

Note that here you start with a number in this long number that is *less* than 12 by a little bit—just as you started with a number that was less than 6 by a little bit. You said 8 × 12 is 96—start with 94; 5 × 12 is 60—start with 58, etc. Note also that the next to last digit is out, but all the others are OK. You will have to multiply the first two end digits of the long new number mentally and then you're all right.

It is best to use the original 5882352941176470 because that will always come out to the last digit.

75. THE MYSTERIOUS BATTLESHIP

Back in 1925, a battleship started from San Francisco on a journey to Tokyo, Japan. One sailor was stationed at the stern, another at the bow, and a third sailor in the "crow's nest," 100 feet up on one of the masts. Assuming

that all three men remained in these positions during the entire trip and did not move until the ship arrived in Tokyo, did all three travel the same distance? If not, which one traveled the farthest?
It might be added that the length of the battleship and the fact that the bow arrived in the dock ahead of the stern have nothing to do with the problem.

76. A VULGAR FRACTION

One-third of a certain fraction, plus three times that fraction, equals that fraction when multiplied by that fraction. Will someone tell us what that fraction is?

77. A LIGHTLY PROBLEM

Two electric light bulbs of 100 watts each are lit and are six inches apart in a ceiling. Will either, neither or both of these bulbs cast a shadow on the walls of the room?

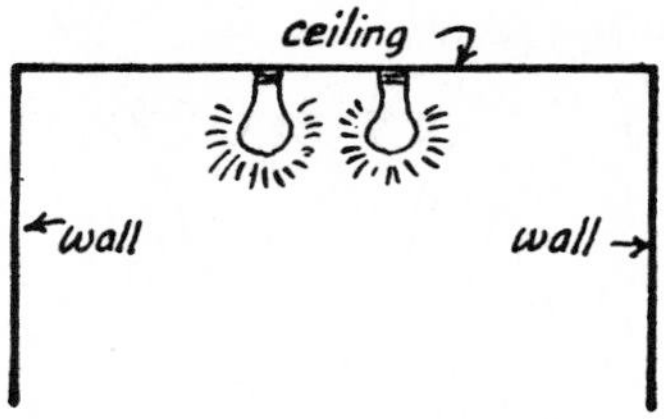

78. FILLING THE WINDOW

This problem seems to be impossible to solve with the flimsy information given, yet it is ridiculously easy. Three squares are inscribed in a circle 34 inches in diameter as shown here. The black square represents a window which has to be filled in. Will a board 12 inches square do the job?

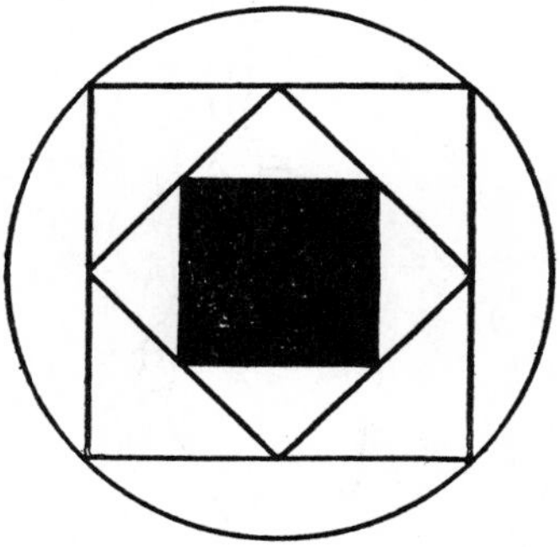

79. I DON'T BELIEVE IT

a. The diagram shows two vessels filled to the same depth with water. The area of the base of vessel A is the same as that of vessel B, yet vessel B holds about 100 times as much water as A. Question: Which base has more weight on it—A or B?

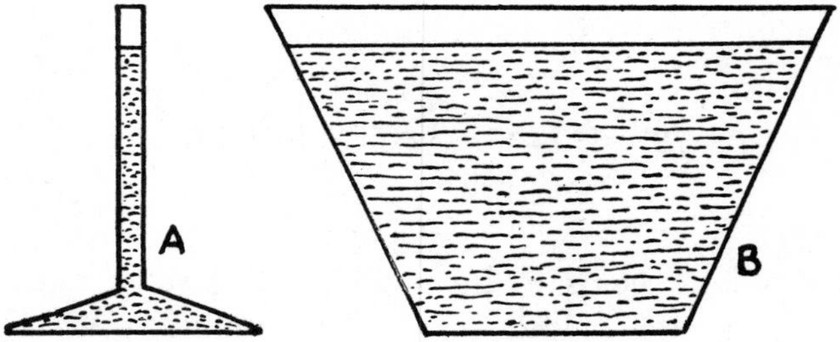

b. If you take the cellophane wrapper off a cigar, hold it in one hand and light one end of it, will the smoke go up or down?

QUIZZES THAT ARE DIFFERENT

80. HOMONYM QUIZ—A. LIVING CREATURES

Homonyms, in case you have forgotten, are words that are pronounced the same but are spelled differently. Right and Write are homonyms and so are Feet and Feat or Meat and Meet. To answer each question below you must fill out *both* words; one will fit the definition, and the other will be the name of some living creature, be it an animal, bird or insect. The answer to No. 10 is BARE-BEAR. What are the others? Par on this is 14 in ten minutes.

1. HUSKY: H_____ and H_____
2. LONG THIN CANDLE: T_____ and T_____
3. TO EXIST: B_____ and B_____
4. TO MAKE A HOLE: B_____ and B_____
5. DID KNOW: K_____ and G_____
6. SECOND PERSON: Y_____ and E_____
7. SLANG FOR MONEY: D_____ and D_____
8. TO FLY AWAY: F_____ and F_____
9. TO ROTATE SLOWLY: T_____ and T_____
10. BARREN: B_____ and B_____
11. PART OF THE HEAD: H_____ and H_____
12. TO COVER: C_____ and S_____
13. A CHILD'S CRY: M_____ and M_____
14. PARTS OF A CHAIN: L_____ and L_____
15. A FURROW: R_____ and R_____
16. A FEMALE RELATIVE: A_____ and A_____
17. GOD OF THE FIELDS: F_____ and F_____
18. EXPENSIVE: D_____ and D_____

19. GAIN BY WORK: E_____ and E_____
20. ROUGHER: C_____ and C_____

81. HOMONYM QUIZ—B. PLANT LIFE

To answer each question below you must fill out both words; one will fit the definition, and the other will be the name of a fruit, plant, vegetable, berry, grain, or it will have to do with some form of plant life. Par for this quiz is 14 in fifteen minutes.

1. TO REMOVE VEGETATION FROM: P_____ and P_____
2. TO GRANT; GIVE UP: C_____ and S_____
3. UNIT OF WEIGHT IN GEMS: C_____ and C_____
4. TO PUNISH BY BLOWS: B_____ and B_____
5. AN ESCAPING OF WATER: L_____ and L_____
6. TO PUT UNDER GROUND: B_____ and B_____
7. LARGE GROUPS OF BIRDS: F_____ and P_____
8. DRESSED PELT OF CERTAIN ANIMALS: F_____ and F_____
9. HAVING TAKEN PLACE: B_____ and B_____
10. VERTICAL: P_____ and P_____
11. A FLOWING ONWARD MOTION: C_____ and C_____
12. A SHORE OF THE SEA: B_____ and B_____
13. OBJECTS PLACED IN NUMEROUS STRAIGHT LINES: R_____ and R_____
14. PERIOD OF DURATION: T_____ and T_____
15. A HIGH-RANKING OFFICER: C_____ and K_____
16. PARTLY BURNED: C_____ and C_____

17. A DEFINITE COURSE TO BE TRAVELED: R_____ and R_____
18. SMALL OBJECT USED IN GOLF: T_____ and T_____
19. GLADLY: WILLINGLY: L_____ and L_____
20. A QUICK DESCENT AS IN A RIVER OR CHANNEL: C_____ and S_____

82. A SUPERSTITIOUS QUIZ IN 13 EASY QUESTIONS

(SUPERSTITIOUS has 13 letters)

If you are superstitious you'll have no trouble with this quiz; if you're not, then it will be a matter of luck with you, so be sure to keep your fingers crossed. How many of these can you complete? Par is 7. Ten or more is excellent. Eight is good and 6 is average. Just complete each sentence:

1. If your nose itches it means that you are _____
2. If you sing before breakfast you'll _____
3. When you return for something you forgot you should _____
4. If your ears itch it is a sure sign that _____
5. If a burning candle has its wick toward you then you_____
6. If you are a girl and you happen to fall upstairs _____
7. If you spill salt you should immediately _____
8. Whenever you boast of good fortune be sure to _____

9. Be glad your right hand itches because it means you ______
10. If someone gives you a knife for a present you must ______
11. If you drop a fork it means that a ______
12. When you see a pin be sure to ______
13. If you should pass a load of hay don't fail to ______

83. ONE AND ONLY QUIZ

If you have ever been in love, and we imagine that most people have, you certainly know the meaning of THE ONE AND ONLY. Of course, no matter how far gone you are you will have to admit that your ONE AND ONLY is a matter of opinion—which is your good luck. But here is a quiz where THE ONE AND ONLY is *not* a matter of opinion. If you can't answer No. 1 you had better go back to Northeastern Siberia. The par for this quiz is 7 correct in ten minutes.

1. The only President who served more than two terms ______
2. The only state which touches only one state is ______
3. The only mammal that has wings and can fly is the ______
4. The only metal that is a liquid at room temperature is ______
5. The only four-letter word when printed in capitals that reads the same upside down as right side up is ______

6. The only star that is bright enough to cast a shadow is ——
7. The only President who was never married was ——
8. The only sure method of identifying a person is through ——
9. The only four-letter word ending in ENY is ——
10. The only prime number that is an even number is ——
11. The only island that is not an island is ——
12. The only four states that meet at right angles are ——
13. The only number whose square equals its square root is ——
14. The only man to be Secretary of War, Chief Justice of the Supreme Court and President of the United States was ——
15. The only place where the Pacific Ocean is east of the Atlantic is at the ——
16. The only continent whose population is less than the population of Denver, Colorado, is ——
17. The only question which cannot be answered truthfully by "No" is ——

84. THE WORLD-FAMOUS PAT PENDING

This fellow Pat Pending seems to have his name on every patented device in America. He knows very well the names of all the inventors that apply to his office but he doesn't always tell. Can you go him one better and tell who invented what, from the following two tables. The par on this is 8, any more than that is excellent. Just pair the name (by number) with the invention (by letter).

1. The fountain pen	a. De Forest
2. Dynamite	b. Mergenthaler
3. The sewing machine	c. Edison
4. The airplane	d. Bell
5. The linotype	e. Hartshorn
6. The phonograph	f. Westinghouse
7. The telephone	g. Marconi
8. The incandescent lamp	h. Nobel
9. Radio vacuum tube triod	i. Wright Bros.
10. Railroad air brake	j. Waterman
11. The window shade roller	k. Whitney
12. Wireless telegraph	l. Howe
13. The saw-type cotton gin	

85. TRIPLET TIME TEST

Here is a fine test against time. The object is to pick out the following triplets by number and write these numbers down in the fastest time. The triplets are three words commonly used together like HOP, SKIP and JUMP or MAN, WOMAN and CHILD. You should be able to do this in four minutes flat. Anything under that is good, and anything under three minutes is excellent. You can play this as a parlor game if you want to, merely by dictating these words to your guests and having them write them down. The answer to the first triplet is 1-6-21 or RED, WHITE and BLUE. One final word: Don't write the words, just write the numbers. Now, READY, GET SET, GO!

1. Red	13. Song	25. Knife
2. Wise	14. Sinker	26. Wealthy
3. Line	15. Wine	27. Fair
4. Woman	16. Barrel	28. Able
5. Look	17. Ready	29. Blood
6. White	18. Listen	30. Hope
7. Lock	19. Forty	31. Healthy
8. Willing	20. Sun	32. Fork
9. Hook	21. Blue	33. Spoon
10. Fat	22. Stock	34. Charity
11. Stop	23. Stars	35. Tears
12. Moon	24. Sweat	36. Faith

86. WHAT'S IN IT TEST

How often do you eat things without having the slightest idea of what is in them? When you chew gum, for example, do you know just what you are chewing? Fill in the blanks with the correct letter which will tell what the object mentioned is made of and score 12½ for each correct answer. There are more ingredients given than there are objects, so you have to be careful to pick the right ones from the list. To start you off we have given you No. 1. Par is 5.

1. By mixing __g__ with __o__ we get dynamite.
2. Chewing gum comes from _____ which is the sap of the _____.
3. Snuff is merely _____.
4. Don't think German silver is silver, it is _____ mixed with _____ and _____.

5. Fine caviar is the _____ of the _____.
6. That delicious marshmallow you ate is made from _____, _____ and _____.
7. If it were not for _____ you would not have tapioca pudding.
8. Most cheese is made from _____.

INGREDIENTS:

a. sturgeon
b. sugar
c. nickel
d. flannel
e. crystal quartz
f. corn syrup
g. nitroglycerine
h. roe
i. sapodilla
j. copper
k. powdered tobacco
l. mica
m. curds
n. lead
o. infusorial earth
p. chicle
q. cassava
r. graphite
s. starch
t. gelatin
u. isinglass
v. cacao
w. zinc
x. tin
y. powdered alum
z. ivory

87. PAIRING CLICHÉS

Wherever you go in this world clichés are always clichés and this test is no exception. The best thing to do with a lot of worn-out sayings like these is to pair them off and get rid of them as fast as you can. Here are 20 of 'em waiting to be paired off and thrown away in record time. Just write the number and the letter after it as shown in 1-e which is obviously "tempt the fates" and keep this up until you have the entire lot paired off. The par on this is three minutes.

1. Tempt
2. Run
3. Take up
4. Gild
5. Cap
6. Toe
7. Throw
8. Shoot
9. Dish
10. Bury
11. Beard
12. Beat about
13. Fly
14. Turn
15. Spill
16. Kick
17. Chew
18. Fill
19. Rush
20. Cut

a. The beans
b. The works
c. The climax
d. The gauntlet
e. The fates
f. The coop
g. The growler
h. The bucket
i. The rag
j. The lily
k. The cudgels
l. The bull
m. The mark
n. The bill
o. The comedy
p. The tables
q. The dirt
r. The hatchet
s. The lion
t. The bush

88. IT AIN'T NECESSARILY SO

The flagman who waves a lantern on a dark night at the railroad crossing is not doing his duty unless that lantern is lit. The same holds true of throwing a match into a kerosense-soaked pile of paper—nothing will happen unless you light the match first. Here is a quiz to test your thinking. Don't jump to conclusions, but think of all possibilities. Of the statements below, some are *always* true and some are not. Can you distinguish which are and which are not? Score 10 for each correct answer. A perfect score is 90; average, 60. Take it easy before checking with the answer page.

1. Anyone who claims to foretell future events with positive certainty is a fake. YES NO
2. If you put your bare finger into a cup filled with coffee, your finger will get wet. YES NO
3. If your fingerprints are the same as those found on a glass then you have touched that glass. YES NO

4. If I can see your eyes in the mirror you can also see mine unless you're blind. YES NO
5. If you jump off the roof of the Empire State Building in New York City, and you fall all the way, you'll be killed. YES NO
6. If a certified check for $10 is certified by a national bank with assets of over $1,000,000, that check is as good as cash. YES NO
7. If you mix a good clear blue paint with a good clear yellow paint the result will be green. YES NO
8. It is a very unseasonable January day if the temperature outside is 90° in the shade. YES NO
9. Anyone born on February 29th can celebrate his true leap-year birthday every four years. YES NO

89. HOW WELL DO YOU KNOW YOUR GADGETS?

Can you decide who uses what in the following quiz. The par for this is 7 correct out of 15.

1. The CASSOCK is for the
   a. Plumber b. Mechanic c. Clergyman

2. The VERNIER is used by the
   a. Surveyor b. Doctor c. Printer

3. The SCALPEL is used by the
   a. Barber b. Surgeon c. Indian

4. The LATHE is used by the
   a. Printer   b. Writer   c. Mechanic

5. The RAMEKINS are for the
   a. Cook   b. Farmer   c. Conductor

6. The PROTRACTOR is used by the
   a. Draftsman   b. Dentist   c. Insurance agent

7. The PODIUM is for the
   a. Policeman   b. Druggist   c. Conductor

8. The GERTRUDE is for the
   a. Infant   b. Movie star   c. Bachelor

9. The THEODOLITE is used by the
   a. Weatherman   b. Engineer   c. Eye doctor

10. The RETORT is used by the
    a. Orator   b. Mortician   c. Chemist

11. The QUADRANT is for the
    a. Upholsterer   b. Mason   c. Mariner

12. The AWL is used by the
    a. Shoemaker   b. Harpist   c. Bookkeeper

13. The TAP is an instrument used by the
    a. Dancer   b. Minister   c. Plumber-mechanic

14. The PANTOGRAPH is used by the
    a. Artist   b. Undertaker   c. Clothing designer

15. The RHEOSTAT is used in
    a. Photography   b. Electric work   c. Medicine

16. A BUSHING is for the
    a. Gardener   b. Mechanic   c. Florist

90. A GAME OF NAMES

All the names listed below are *first* names of men, but most of them happen to be last names too. For example, the famous outlaw Jesse James had two names each of which is a man's first name. By matching names from this list you should be able to put together 15 pairs, each pair being the first and last name of some well-known person living or dead. To start you off we'll tell you that the first one is 1-23, or Benjamin Franklin. What are the rest? Par is 7 pairs correct in 2 minutes.

1. Benjamin
2. William
3. Arthur
4. Douglas
5. Fred
6. Marshall
7. John
8. James
9. Louis
10. George
11. Benny
12. Stephen
13. Joe
14. Gilbert
15. Irving
16. Henry
17. Allen
18. Walter
19. Jack
20. Leslie
21. Chester
22. Milton
23. Franklin
24. Washington
25. Bruno
26. Thomas
27. Jerome
28. Jerome
29. Howard
30. Patrick

91. HOW'S YOUR ETIQUETTE?

Have you brushed up on your etiquette lately, or are you just instinctively an etiquette fan? Do you know exactly the right thing to say at the right time, and how to enter a roomful of people without making everyone nervous? Most of us know the little things that make us "socially acceptable" . . . things like rising when a woman comes into the room or removing one's hat in the house, but what about the borderline cases? If you come out with more than 8 correct you can be sure that Boston's best will beat a path to your door.

1. The proper introduction is:
   a. Miss A meet Mr. B. b. This is Mr. B, Mary. c. Miss A, may I present Mr. B.

2. Acknowledge an introduction with:
   a. Glad to know you. b. Pleased to meet you. c. How do you do?

3. A man removes his hat in:
   a. Business building elevator. b. A department store elevator. c. An apartment house elevator.

4. Mr. and Mrs. John Doe register at a hotel as:
   a. Mr. and Mrs. John Doe. b. John Doe and wife. c. John B. and Jane R. Doe.

5. Jane Doe signs herself:
   a. Jane R. Doe. b. Jane R. Doe (Mrs. J. B.). c. Mrs. John Doe.

6. When a couple becomes engaged congratulate:
   a. The man. b. The girl. c. Both.

7. When speaking of your spouse to a social equal say:
   a. Mr. Jones says. . . . b. John says. . . . c. My husband says. . . .

8. Which of the following may be eaten with the fingers:

a. Corn b. Olives c. Potato chips d. Pickles e. Artichokes f. Crisp bacon g. Pie h. Berries

9. A bread-and-butter letter should be written:
   a. Within two weeks b. Within 24 hours c. At any time

10. A man should always rise when:
    a. A woman employee enters his office. b. A woman visitor enters. c. The cleaning woman enters.

11. If a man meets a girl friend eating lunch in a restaurant he should:
    a. Let her pay for her lunch. b. Pay for her lunch. c. Let her pay for his lunch.

12. My wife and widowed mother have the same names. How should they be distinguished?

92. WINING, DINING AND RHYMING

Are you ever embarrassed when you take your girl to a swell French restaurant and you see all those French names on the menu? How sure are you that you can pronounce them and toss them off at the *garçon* with a nonchalance that would make the Duke of Windsor envious? Here is a test to tell you how good or bad you are. Pronounce the French word correctly in each of the couplets below and select the proper word in the second line to rhyme with it. Total, 100; par is 60.

1. A most particular *gourmet*
   Was sitting in a small (café—luncheonette).
2. The chef was proud of his *cuisine*
   And always kept things looking (fine—clean).
3. There was a very small *couvert.*
   It wasn't large enough to (hurt—scare).
4. We started on an *apéritif*
   Before we even had our (beef—knife).
5. And then we chose a *table d'hôte*
   Of which the waiter made a (jot—note).
6. Our first selection was *hors d'oeuvres.*
   This order they made haste to (cover—serve).
7. And then we order *consommé*
   In which there was a taste of (bay—rum).
8. We next enjoyed some fine *poulet*
   Which, as you know, is rare (to get—today).
9. We topped it off with a *meringue*
   To give our meal an extra (tang—fling).
10. We did not have *café au lait*
    Because our waiter did not (wait—stay).

93. ARE YOU AN OBSERVANT SHOPPER?

This quiz will test your powers of observation as a shopper. Here are fourteen trade marks of nationally advertised products, many of which you buy every day. How many of these can you identify? You should be able to get at least eight correct to qualify as an observant shopper.

1. A nut in top hat and spats.
2. A rosy-cheeked kid in a chef's outfit.
3. A girl with an umbrella in the rain.
4. A smiling devil with a pitchfork.
5. The numbers "10 - 2 - 4" arranged in a circle.
6. Three intersecting circles.
7. Two men with long beards.
8. An eagle halfway through the letter A.
9. An empty inverted cup with a single drop coming from it.
10. A happy cow with a necklace of flowers.
11. A kindly colonial gentleman in a broad-brimmed hat.
12. A house in the woods with a smoking chimney.
13. A happy young girl smiling under a bonnet.
14. A friendly tiger in a neckerchief.

94. HOW GOOD IS YOUR MEMORY?

How good is your memory of events? Of course we know you can't name the day, month and year that certain events took place—not one in a thousand can do that—but how about the sequence of events? Surely you know that Prohibition ended before World War II began; that's easy, and so are some of the following. All you have to do is to letter the three events in their correct sequence. The answer to No. 1 is b c a. What are the others? Par for this is 5 out of 10. Anything above that is very good.

1. a. Japan surrenders
   b. Germany surrenders
   c. The atom bomb hits Hiroshima
2. a. Germany invades Russia
   b. The Dionne Quintuplets are born
   c. The Atlantic Charter Conference
3. a. Roosevelt dies
   b. The Potsdam Conference
   c. England declares war on Germany
4. a. The Munich pact
   b. Hitler named Chancellor
   c. Marshall becomes Secretary of State
5. a. The Yalta Conference
   b. The Cairo Conference
   c. The Casablanca Conference
6. a. The Stock Market collapse
   b. The Lindbergh baby is kidnaped
   c. The National Bank Holiday
7. a. V-J Day
   b. June 14, 1945
   c. The first San Francisco Conference
8. a. Holland invaded by Germany
   b. Belgium surrendered
   c. Norway invaded by Germany
9. a. LaGuardia dies
   b. Gandhi dies
   c. Princess Elizabeth marries
10. a. Nazi gang executed
    b. The Truman Doctrine
    c. The Marshall Plan

95. LOW SCORE QUIZ

The object is to answer as many of the following *wrong* as you can. This is not easy to do and the one with the greatest number of *wrong answers* wins. Par is 8 wrong answers.

Answer the following questions *wrong:*

1. How many stars are there in the American flag: 64 or 50?

2. Which was the first day of the Twentieth Century: January 1, 1900 or January 1, 1901?
3. Which is nearer the earth: the sun or the moon?
4. Is a peanut a nut or a vegetable?
5. Which city is nearer Rio de Janeiro, South America: El Paso, Texas, or Montreal, Canada?
6. Who was the first Emperor of Rome: Caesar or Augustus?
7. Is Tegucigalpa a tropical city or a tropical plant?
8. Is there such a thing as a solid chunk of metal that will float on water? Yes or No.
9. Panama City is: in the Canal Zone or outside the Canal Zone?
10. Which President served more than two terms: Theodore Roosevelt or Franklin D. Roosevelt?
11. Which city is west of Los Angeles: Carson City, Nevada, or San Bernardino, California?
12. Is a blind worm another name for a mole? Yes or No.
13. Which is the correct date of Washington's Birthday: February 11, 1732, or February 22, 1732?
14. Which do you give a druggist: a prescription or a perscription?
15. Is a half dozen dozen the same as six dozen dozen? Yes or No.
16. If I mix a pint of water with a pint of alcohol will I have a quart of liquid? Yes or No.

96. CHARADE QUIZ

The Robinsons acted out a number of clever charades the other evening. Before each charade the guests were told the number of syllables in the word and its initial letter, and it was for them to guess that word from what the host or hostess did. The host, for example, sighed loudly and then started to kick vigorously. He then told everyone it was a word beginning with P with two syllables. The answer, of course, is PSYCHIC or sigh—kick. Although you were not at that Robinson party we think you will have a lot of fun with these charades, and you can also use this list at your next party. Here is what the host and hostess did:

1. The host held an ice cube in each hand and then started to press them together. (2 syllables beginning with P)

2. The hostess appeared with a hair net in her hand. She then threw the net as far as she could. (3 syllables beginning with C)

3. The host showed a bottle of chili sauce and placed it very close to the edge of a card table. (2 syllables beginning with S)

4. The hostess took over. She held up a can of soup, rouged her lips, powdered her nose, pretended to make up her eyebrows and then assumed an obvious pose. (4 syllables beginning with S)

5. A startling charade followed. The host held a large 8 above his head and set it on fire. (3 syllables beginning with H)

6. The hostess now showed everyone a sign as follows: XwvutsrqponmlkjihgfedC (3 syllables beginning with E)

7. The host held up a package of tea saying, "This is a more recent brand of tea." (4 syllables beginning with A)

8. The hostess entered the room, knocked on a door, turned around and went right out again. (2 syllables beginning with N)

9. The host and hostess did this one together. Hostess pretended to faint and host brought her to. The hostess then said, "My dear nephew, I am ever so grateful for reviving me." (3 syllables beginning with R)

10. The host entered with a block of wood in which there is a large nail. He pulled at it for a while and then said, "I guess that nail is in there and won't come out."

11. The hostess showed everyone two very frail letters, S and N, which she had cut from tissue. She handled them very carefully and announced that they were very easily torn. (5 syllables beginning with D)

12. The host held up a fountain pen and then he held up the ten of spades. Finally he showed everyone a bottle of sherry. (5 syllables beginning with P)

13. The hostess now showed everyone a huge letter S which she had printed on a big sheet of cardboard. (2 syllables beginning with L)

14. In this charade the hostess shook hands with the host and said, "How do you do, doctor, I'm certainly glad I met you." (5 syllables beginning with M)

15. For the last charade the host held up a penny and shouted ten times. (3 syllables beginning with C)

97. SLICED HAM QUIZ

Here is a brand-new quiz and game at the same time. You can try it solo first and then play it at your next party. Give out pencils and paper and tell everyone to write the words SLICED HAM at the top of their papers. Now read the following definitions and allow two minutes between each definition. It is required to write a six-letter word fitting the definition and, at the same time, using only the letters in the words SLICED HAM. No other letters are allowed and no letter can be used more than once. Here is an example:

DEFINITION: desert animals ANSWER: Camels

Here are the others:

DEFINITIONS:

1. A carpenter's tool — — — — — —
2. Cheerless; mournful — — — — — —
3. Common way to serve potatoes — — — — — —
4. To protect; guard — — — — — —
5. Enmity; bad will — — — — — —
6. Put in the postbox — — — — — —
7. What gentlemen go for — — — — — —
8. Followed or pursued — — — — — —
9. A set of large bells in action — — — — — —
10. Converted into money — — — — — —
11. Demands on legal grounds — — — — — —
12. Small metal discs as rewards — — — — — —

98. THAT'S RIGHT, YOU'RE WRONG—1

The object of this quiz is to get you all mixed up so you will have to be on your guard all the time. Some of the statements and questions seem to be correct and are not, while others seem to be wrong and are correct. Just follow directions and take your time. If you answer more than 6 the way they should be answered you are to be congratulated.

1. Answer this wrong: Do bees gather honey from flowers? Yes ☐ No ☐
2. Answer this correctly: Is there a country between France and Spain? Yes ☐ No ☐
3. Answer this correctly: Does the compass needle point to the North Pole? Yes ☐ No ☐
4. Answer this wrong: Did Eve tempt Adam with an apple? Yes ☐ No ☐
5. Answer this wrong: Which number is not a perfect square? 64 ☐ 48 ☐
6. Answer this wrong: Did the Wright brothers build the first airplane? Yes ☐ No ☐
7. Answer this correctly: The term "midsummer" refers to the middle of summer. Yes ☐ No ☐
8. Answer this correctly: Is it wise to keep all acids away from the eyes? Yes ☐ No ☐
9. Answer this wrong: Meteorology is the study of meteors. Yes ☐ No ☐
10. Answer this correctly: Is Lincoln's portrait on the $10 bill? Yes ☐ No ☐

99. WHO'S WHO

We recently attended a party at which everyone had a fine time talking on subjects which did or did not have to do with his or her profession or vocation. An actuary was talking about insurance statistics, which was just what he should be talking about, but when the cattyman started talking about cattle I knew he didn't know much about the subject. Can you straighten these people out for me and tell me who is discussing a subject foreign to his profession or vocation and who is talking shop? Par is 7.

1. Dick Tucker, the ophthalmologist, gave a lecture on birds.
2. Phil Daly, the cartographer, talked about old wagons.
3. Joe Burns, the orthodontist, discussed jaw formations.
4. Jim Briggs, the Savoyard, gave a talk on ancient diseases.
5. Bill Smythe, a bushelman, talked about barreling fruit.
6. Harry Owens, pediatrician, discussed diseases of the feet.
7. Rowland Peters, osteopath, told about bone manipulation.
8. Jerry Waters, an enthusiastic philatelist, bored everyone for an hour on the subject of stamps.
9. Jesse Moore, ornithologist, discussed dentistry with a pretty young college girl.
10. Peter Wolf, the young paleontologist, told us all about fossils.

Which of these men, by number, talked shop and what

should the others talk about to be within their respective professions and vocations?

100. JUST LOOK AROUND A BIT

If you were asked what it says on the lid of a postbox you undoubtedly would say, "U. S. Mail." It doesn't say that at all. It says, "PULL DOWN." You do a lot of phoning and yet it is unlikely that you know on which side of a pay telephone the coin return is located. Not one person in fifty can tell the kind of taxi he just got into or the make of the elevator in his apartment. Everyone sees things; few people observe things. For this reason the following quiz is more of a guessing contest than a quiz. If you get more than five correct you are either unusually observant or just plain lucky.

1. Do you go out at night much? If so, is the full moon high or low at midnight in a December sky?
2. You use your car a lot—what is the license number?
3. Does the Statue of Liberty have her right or her left hand raised?
4. In your city or town is the red traffic light above the green?
5. You certainly look at money a great deal. Is Washington facing to your right or your left on the dollar bill?
6. Play a lot of gin rummy? Which king has no mustache on the standard playing cards?
7. Most people shop at the A & P. Can you tell what that company's full name is?
8. If you live in a private house, can you tell approximately how many steps you have been walking up or down between the first and second floors?
9. In any book is page 121 a right-hand page or a left-

hand page?

10. Is the hot-water faucet in a basin to your right or your left as you face it?

101. A REAL NOSY QUIZ

The following are definitions for some figures of speech involving noses. No. 1, for example, is NOSED OUT. What are the others? Par is 12 in 4 minutes.

1. Defeated by a narrow margin
2. Very obvious
3. Precisely
4. Disdain
5. Control absolutely
6. A reformer
7. Be very industrious
8. A bunch of flowers
9. Pay an exorbitant price
10. Tally those present
11. To move in a fixed direction
12. Prying or inquisitive
13. Make a person unpopular
14. A speedy vertical descent
15. To make a foolish or harmful suggestion

102. UNITED STATES MAP QUIZ

How is your "map sense" and your sense of direction? If it is good you will score very well on this quiz and if it is poor you'll soon find out what is wrong with it. Just group the following cities or states in their correct location about the city or state named at the right. Remember that east is always at the right, west is at the left, north is above and south is below. Just write the numbers corresponding to the states or cities as shown in the first example. Michigan

(2) is north (above) of Indiana; Ohio (3) is east (to the right) of Indiana; Illinois (4) is west (to the left) of Indiana; and Kentucky (1) is south (below) of Indiana. Fill in the others. Par is 3.

A.

1. Kentucky
2. Michigan
3. Ohio
4. Illinois

	2	
4	INDIANA	3
	1	

B.

1. Indianapolis
2. Toledo
3. Milwaukee
4. Omaha

CHICAGO

C.

1. Oklahoma
2. Colorado
3. Missouri
4. Nebraska

KANSAS

D.

1. Huntington
2. Pittsburgh
3. Detroit
4. Indianapolis

COLUMBUS, OHIO

E.

1. Montana
2. Colorado
3. Utah
4. Nebraska

WYOMING

F.

1. St. Louis
2. Jackson
3. Little Rock
4. Chattanooga

MEMPHIS, TENNESSEE

G.

1. Minnesota
2. Nebraska
3. Illinois
4. Missouri

IOWA

H.

1. St. Louis
2. Omaha
3. Denver
4. Tulsa, Oklahoma

KANSAS CITY

103. HOW WELL DO YOU MIX?

This is a quiz on mixing or combining and will show whether or not you are a good mixer. Just choose one of the three answers below each combination and if you get more than six correct you are a fine mixer.

1. The mixture of copper and zinc gives:
    a. bronze
    b. pewter
    c. brass
2. Mix yellow paint with blue and get:
    a. brown
    b. green
    c. gray

3. Mate a jackass with a mare and the offspring is a:
   a. mule
   b. donkey
   c. zebra
4. Combine two parts hydrogen with one part oxygen and get:
   a. water
   b. air
   c. nitrogen
5. When lead and tin are mixed the alloy is called:
   a. type metal
   b. bronze
   c. solder
6. When a green light is thrown on a red light the result is:
   a. yellow
   b. white
   c. orange
7. A mixture of oxygen and nitrogen gives us:
   a. water
   b. ammonia
   c. air
8. The Oriental and English languages mix to make:
   a. pig Latin
   b. Esperanto
   c. pidgin English
9. A mixture of copper and tin gives:
   a. bronze
   b. pewter
   c. brass
10. Combine the musical notes C, E and A and you get:
   a. a discord
   b. pleasing chord
   c. a noise

11. Half woman and half a fish gives:
    a. a mermaid
    b. a centaur
    c. a satyr
12. A combination of iron and carbon gives us:
    a. pewter
    b. steel
    c. gun metal

104. GENERAL QUIZ

Here are a variety of questions that need answering. Some of them are easy and some are really tough. If you get more than 8 right you are to be congratulated.

1. What word ending in ICT does *not* rhyme with the word CONVICT?
2. An ibis, an ibex and an ibid were all fleeing a hunter. Which ran, which crawled and which flew?
3. Can you think of a word of nine letters which has only one vowel in it?
4. What girl's name of six letters spells the same backwards as it does forwards?
5. There are many words containing double o's or double n's, but can you mention a word with a double w?
6. What is the only city in this hemisphere where the noon sun is directly overhead on June 21st?
7. Which one of the following operas was written by Wagner: a. *The Flying Dutchman* b. *William Tell* c. *Hansel and Gretel*
8. An American hunter with only one bullet in his gun

met a panther, a puma and a mountain lion. How did he save himself?

9. Although it is generally considered an abbreviation it has become a common three-letter word without any vowels in it. What is it?
10. Will a solid steel ball, one inch in diameter, sink in all liquids?
11. What young animal is called a "pup" though its father is a bull and its mother is a cow?
12. What two words of three letters each, pronounced the same but spelled differently, refer to wild life? One has to do with animals and the other has to do with trees.

105. COLLECTOR'S ITEMS

Below you will see two columns. The second contains the names of American cities and the first contains the items for which these cities are famous. Of course the items are all mixed up and you must pair off the city with its particular product by number and letter. The answer to No. 1, for example, is 1-e since film is associated with Eastman in Rochester, N. Y., and Rochester is known as the Kodak city. What are the others? Par: 11.

1. Color film	a. Niagara Falls, N. Y.
2. A new car	b. Washington, D. C.
3. A bottle of Schlitz	c. Hartford, Conn.
4. Pandas	d. Saratoga, N. Y.
5. A suite of furniture	e. Rochester, N. Y.
6. Gambling chips	f. Detroit, Mich.
7. A pass to a movie house	g. Indianapolis, Ind.

8. A timepiece	h. Hershey, Pa.
9. A bean pot	i. Hollywood, Calif.
10. Racing cars	j. Grand Rapids, Mich.
11. The shreds of a $2 racing ticket	k. Elgin, Ill.
12. An insurance policy	l. Boston, Mass.
13. A chocolate bar	m. Battle Creek, Mich.
14. An old shoe and some rice	n. Las Vegas, Nev.
15. A sack of flour	o. Milwaukee, Wis.
16. A box of breakfast food	p. St. Paul, Minn.

106. NICKNAMES, PAST AND PRESENT

Here is a list of famous people of the past and the present, all of whom have well-known nicknames. How many of these nicknames can you supply? The par for this is 12.

1. Jack Dempsey _____	11. Frank Sinatra _____
2. F. H. LaGuardia _____	12. Luis Firpo _____
3. William Cody _____	13. Calvin Coolidge _____
4. Lou Gehrig _____	14. Leo Durocher _____
5. Al Smith _____	15. Sigmund Spaeth _____
6. Joe Louis _____	16. Huey Long _____
7. John Barrymore _____	17. Babe Ruth _____
8. General Patton _____	18. Charles Lindbergh ___
9. Mary Pickford _____	19. Joe Namath _____
10. Will Rogers _____	20. Jimmy Durante _____

107. WHAT'S IN A REAL NAME?

In this unusual quiz we give you a very short description of a famous person together with his or her real name and it is for you to tell who that person is by giving the name by which he or she is generally known. To take a typical example, William Cody, the person described in No. 1 is generally known as Buffalo Bill. Who are the others? Par: 7.

1. An American scout and showman from Iowa who was born in 1846 and whose real name was William F. Cody.
2. An American novelist and humorist born in Missouri, 1835. His real name was Samuel Langhorne Clemens.
3. English instructor of mathematics who wrote two classics for children and whose real name was Charles Dodgson.
4. Famous Canadian actress by the name of Gladys Smith. She won the hearts of everyone in the days of the silent films.
5. A great short-story writer, born in North Carolina in 1862, by the name of William Sydney Porter.
6. A great American actress who made the name of Tillie famous and whose real name was Lelia Doerber.
7. A French novelist whose real name (or names) was Amantine Lucile Aurore Dudevant. She enjoyed listening to Chopin.
8. An English novelist who wrote many remarkable sea stories and whose real name was Jozef Korzeniowski.
9. A little fellow by the name of Charles Stratton who made a great hit first in England and then in this country back in the middle eighties.
10. A great singer and entertainer, whose name was Isidore Baline.

108. AN AMERIQUIZ

This little quiz is not designed to test your knowledge of American history, but is made up of odds and ends that are or should be well known about this country. Most of these were once known but forgotten, so if you score well here it shows you have a good memory or you are just plain lucky.

1. How many stripes were there in the original Stars and Stripes?
2. Who was known as Stonewall Jackson: Andrew Jackson or Thomas Jackson?
3. On what island was the famous flag raising done in World War II?
4. What is wrong with this: "O thus be it ever that freedom shall stand between our loved homes and the war's desolation"?
5. Give the name of the song and the verse number of the quotation in No. 4.
6. Coolidge, Teddy Roosevelt, Chester Arthur, Van Buren, Andrew Johnson and Millard Fillmore were all in a club in Heaven. Why was F.D.R. refused membership?
7. How are the 50 stars arranged in the U.S. flag?
8. Which is the most southerly city in the United States?

9. A traveling salesman visited Buffalo, Cleveland, Columbus, Indianapolis, Chicago, Denver, Seattle, Boise, Cheyenne and Lincoln, Nebraska. How many state capitals did he visit and what are they?
10. On what hill was the Battle of Bunker Hill fought?

109. TO BE SHOERE

The following are definitions of some expressions involving feet, parts of feet or footwear. No. 1, for example, is COLD FEET. What are the others? Par: 10.

1. If you wish to back out of a promise or an agreement because you fear the consequences you have ________
2. If you sit around an office for hours waiting for an interview and you feel you are wasting your time you are said to be ________
3. If you say something you shouldn't have said and, as a consequence, you get into trouble you have ________
4. If you are alert and eager and seize every opportunity to take advantage of a situation you are ________
5. If a person always looks sick and goes around complaining of his health we say he has ________
6. When a spoiled and unruly child is placed in the care of a strict schoolmaster, that schoolmaster will make the child ________
7. He's a drip, he's a jerk, he's a flat tire—he's a ________
8. When some misfortune which happens to others and which you have shown little interest in actually happens to you, then the ________

9. When I say that I would not like to be in the predicament that you find yourself in I say I would ________
10. If you worry and fret over some future event that may mean trouble for you, you are said to ________
11. When you are free to travel and have no responsibilities whatever you are ________
12. An obsequious person is one who, according to the saying, might ________
13. When you get something extra thrown in on an apparent bargain you get that thing ________
14. If you want to make a good impression and you have something to sell you start by ________
15. You marry an heiress but you don't want her folks to support you because you want to show them that you can ________
16. When a man starts in business with only $5.00 and succeeds in making a fortune we say he ________

110. LIST AND LEARN QUIZ

This is really more of a game than a quiz for the individual. The best way to play this is to give your guests pencils and paper and read each question to them, allowing at least two minutes between questions to list the various items. You can make up your own scoring remembering that it must be done on a percentage basis using each question separately. If Miss Peters, for example, gets 5 correct out of 8 on a question she will score 62½ percent on that particular question. The average scores can be computed later. Here are the questions:

1. Name the Seven Wonders of the Ancient World.
2. Name the five Great Lakes. (Double credit for naming them in correct order of size.)
3. Name the nine planets of the solar system.
4. List 8 of the 12 signs of the zodiac.
5. Name 6 of the largest states (in area) in the continental United States. (Double credit for listing in order of size.)
6. Name the four Beatles.
7. List 8 of the largest cities (in population) in the United States. (Double credit for listing in order of size.)
8. Name the 10 Presidents who served before Jimmy Carter in reverse order.
9. Name 8 countries in South America.
10. Name 13 Vice Presidents who became President.

111. QUIZ OF THE MONTHS—A

Even if you do not score high on the following quizzes you are sure to find out many things that you have either forgotten or did not know about the various months. If you get a high score you can be sure that you know more than most people. This is more of an information quiz than a test, hence there is no par.

1. How did January get its name?
2. A certain date in January marked the beginning of everything evil. What is that date?
3. When is Twelfth Night and what does it celebrate?
4. When is ground-hog day and what happens on it?

5. Name two famous men who were born on the same day in the same year in the month of February.
6. Thomas A. Edison was born on February 11th in which year: 1835 1847 1881
7. Spring comes about March 21st. What happens at that time?
8. How did March get its name?
9. How is Easter determined?
10. What does the name "April" mean?
11. How did April Fools' Day originate?
12. Give three well-known quotations which mention April.
13. For what purpose was Memorial Day originated and who started it?
14. How did the Maypole get its start?
15. Who originated Mother's Day and when was the first Mother's Day?

112. QUIZ OF THE MONTHS—B

1. What is June 6th?
2. What anniversary is celebrated on June 14th?
3. Summer comes officially about June 21st. How do astronomers determine the entrance of summer?
4. What was the month of July originally called by the Romans?
5. When is St. Swithin's Day and what is the fable about?
6. What epoch-making event took place on July 28th?
7. What was the exact date of the signing of the Declaration of Independence?
8. How did August get its name?

9. What great commercial event took place on August 15th?
10. What great event took place on August 14th?
11. What happened on August 5, 1945?
12. When is Labor Day and how did it come to be a holiday?
13. What is meant by the autumnal equinox?
14. How did September get its name?
15. What great event took place on September 3rd?

113. QUIZ OF THE MONTHS—C

1. Two dates in October celebrate the discovery of America. One is easy but what is the other date?
2. Just when is Halloween and why witches and spooks?
3. When is Navy Day?
4. Is Election Day always the first Tuesday in November?
5. Where and at what hour was the Armistice of World War I signed?
6. Just what does Thanksgiving celebrate?
7. Why the turkey as a symbol of Thanksgiving?
8. Where does the name "November" come from?
9. About when is the first day of winter and what happens on that day?
10. How did Christmas get its name?
11. How did Santa Claus get his name?
12. Why do we exchange gifts on Christmas?
13. What happened in New York City on December 26, 1947?
14. Is every year that is divisible by 4 a leap year?

114. ANIMAL SYMPHONY OPUS 1

If a dog barks and a cat meows, what words are used to describe the sounds made by other living creatures? It is for you to fill these in with the common word used to describe the sound made by that living creature. No. 1 has been done for you. What are the others? Score 5 for each correct answer. Par is 90.

1. CAT Meows purrs
2. DOG
3. HORSE
4. OWL
5. HEN
6. PIG
7. GOOSE
8. DUCK
9. WOLF
10. FROG
11. LAMB
12. SEAL
13. TURKEY
14. SNAKE
15. CROW
16. BULL
17. DOVE
18. LION
19. DONKEY
20. MONKEY
21. SPARROW
22. BABY CHICK
23. ROOSTER
24. MAGPIE
25. HYENA
26. YOUNG PUPPY
27. ELEPHANT
28. BEAR
29. COW
30. RAVEN

115. LIVING CREATURES QUIZ

The following are definitions of common expressions involving living creatures. Just name the animal or bird or reptile indicated in each expression. No. 1, for example, is WOLF. To keep the *wolf* from the door. What are the others? (Give the expressions, if you can.) Par: 14.

1. To earn enough to keep from starvation.
2. A mean, low, contemptible person.
3. A driver who wants the entire road to himself.
4. A short, light sleep.
5. Foolish pranks.
6. A great social success idolized by the girls.
7. To imitate.
8. To overawe someone; to inspire fear in him.
9. A person who tries to impress one by cringing.
10. To boast loudly over a particular accomplishment.
11. Unusually large.
12. Gross exaggeration; bragging about things that are not so.
13. A comedian whose antics are boisterous, loud and obvious.
14. A jargon imitating Latin.
15. Hoarseness.
16. A frolic or merry adventure.
17. What you do to a letter before posting it.
18. A person who lacks courage; a weak, cowardly person.

116. INTRODUCTORY VOCABULARY QUIZ

Here are 20 sentences with one word left blank in each sentence. Below these sentences are 20 words which are numbered and it is up to you to place the correct word in each sentence by its number. Average is 9; 16 is excellent and anything more than 18 is exceptional. No. 1 is done for you.

1. His plan is still in the 7 stage.
2. I can't afford to dine with her, her tastes are too —.
3. This detective mystery is far too — to be popular.
4. He claims that his new theories will be a — for the country.
5. She regarded him with a critical and — air.
6. That recent tidal wave was a devastating —.
7. I take that last remark as a personal —.
8. There she sat, looking coy, — and shy.
9. Each young actor tried his best to — Barrymore.
10. Helen has a strong — to cats.
11. He has a superficial knowledge of the arts and is a —.
12. Anyone who is — is sure to be wasteful.
13. A — solution will put you to sleep.
14. A cruel person is often —.
15. If she does little talking she is —.
16. — are laws that are passing out of existence.
17. During a war there is a — of civilian nurses.
18. He is far from taciturn, in fact he is quite —.
19. That crime is — to murder.
20. He exhibits sudden — outbursts of temper.

1. Supercilious	7. Embryonic	13. Dilettante
2. Macabre	8. Panacea	14. Soporific
3. Cataclysm	9. Demure	15. Taciturn
4. Paucity	10. Antipathy	16. Spasmodic
5. Tantamount	11. Emulate	17. Profligate
6. Epicurean	12. Sadistic	18. Loquacious
19. Moribund	20. Affront	

117. VOCABULARY QUIZ—A

Listed below are fifteen sentences with appropriate descriptions for the underscored words. If you get more than 12 correct your vocabulary is excellent; more than 9 it is good and anything under 6 it is poor.

1. If you met a *chauvinist* you would expect him to:
   a. rave over G. B. Shaw b. be patriotic c. do tricks for you
2. A certain *Alpine goat* is known as an:
   a. ibis b. ibex c. ibid
3. *Tautology* is the:
   a. study of stress and strain b. study of ocean life c. repetition of words in close succession
4. A *miter* box is a box which:
   a. holds incense b. is used by carpenters c. holds valuables
5. If you studied *ceramics* you would be studying:
   a. clay modeling and baking b. history c. acting
6. If someone presented you with a *dory* you would:
   a. feed it b. drive it in open country c. row on the lake with it
7. What would you do with a case of *impetigo?*
   a. sell it b. drink the contents c. call a doctor
8. If he is *cantankerous* he is:
   a. mean b. susceptible to colds c. double-jointed

9. A *misanthrope* is:
   a. a hopeless drunkard b. a hater of mankind c. a stamp collector
10. You would look for a *vixen* in:
   a. a hardware store b. the woods c. a church
11. If something is *esculent* it is:
   a. edible b. hollow c. difficult to handle
12. Anything that is *crass* is:
   a. made of grass or reeds b. absolutely true c. coarse
13. A *pundit* is a person who:
   a. is very wise b. is always making puns c. is nobly born
14. A *plenipotentiary* is:
   a. a reformatory b. a measure of weight c. a diplomat
15. You arouse my *ire* when:
   a. you lift my arm b. make me curious c. make me angry

118. VOCABULARY QUIZ—B

Underline the word or words which best define the words in italics. Fourteen or more correct is excellent; 12 is good and 10 is average.

1. If Roland is greedy and *miserly* he is:
   a. didactic b. irascible c. avaricious
2. If you *hate* mathematics it is:
   a. your forte b. your bête noire c. a fetish with you
3. Eva is extremely *skillful* in her work. She is:
   a. phlegmatic b. adroit c. acrimonious

4. If you travel *incognito* you travel:
a. in luxury b. in haste c. in disguise
5. If you did something *with impunity* you:
a. did it well b. escaped punishment c. did it poorly
6. Stanley's speech is filled with *platitudes,* consequently:
a. he's a bore b. he uses big words c. he scintillates
7. If something is done *sub rosa* it is done:
a. with ceremony b. in confidence c. underground
8. If you always act with *extreme caution* you are:
a. sadistic b. circumspect c. desultory
9. If I gave my home a *cursory* cleaning I:
a. did a thorough job b. did it unwillingly c. did it hastily
10. If Mary is *needlessly concerned about her health* she is:
a. a hypochondriac b. a paranoiac c. a somnambulist
11. If you studied *orthodontia* you studied:
a. birds b. teeth c. religion
12. If you are on the *qui vive* you're:
a. alert b. secretive c. nervous
13. A person who knows a lot about *facets* is:
a. a plumber b. a tinsmith c. a jeweler
14. If you are interested in *histrionics* you should be:
a. an historian b. an actor c. a mechanic
15. Little Jane is *petulant,* consequently she is:
a. affectionate b. stupid c. sulky
16. An *anomaly* is:
a. an exaggeration b. a white flower c. an irregularity

119. UP-TO-THE-MINUTE ENGLISH

During the last 25 years most of the following words have become part of our language. How many of them can you define with reasonable accuracy? Average is 16; 22 is excellent and anything more than 22 is exceptional. Here we go:

1. Video
2. Stuka
3. Rightist
4. Bazooka
5. Cyclotron
6. Bobby-soxer
7. Goon
8. Jive
9. Kamikaze
10. Jalopy
11. Roger
12. Gremlins
13. Walkie-talkie
14. Commando
15. Neptunium
16. Jeep
17. Quisling
18. Fellow traveler
19. Snafu
20. Fission
21. Iconoscope
22. Spitfire
23. Blitz
24. Schneid
25. Hostels
26. Positron
27. Plutonium
28. Dynatron
29. Stereo
30. Polaroid
31. Lulu
32. Sputnik

120. TROUBLESOME PLURALS

The plural of most words is easy to form, but some words —particularly compound words—are very tricky and don't seem to have any system of forming plurals. Here are thirty toughies. If you get more than 20 correct you're marvelous. Par for this quiz is 12.

Write the plurals of:

1. Daughter-in-law
2. Attorney general
3. Brigadier general
4. Judge advocate
5. Chargé d'affaires
6. Potato
7. Notary public
8. Law merchant
9. Opus
10. Pelvis
11. Sergeant major
12. Teaspoonful
13. Piccolo
14. Table d'hôte
15. Court-martial
16. Paymaster general
17. Mister
18. Madam
19. Crisis
20. Man-of-war
21. Lieutenant colonel
22. Bandit
23. Cannon
24. Phenomenon
25. Aviatrix
26. Manservant
27. Oboe
28. Ox
29. Valet de chambre
30. Datum

WORD PUZZLES

DUO-WORD TESTS

There are thousands of words that are made up of shorter words which have nothing whatever to do with the original word itself. Take, for example, the word ANTHEM. This is composed of two three-letter words, ANT and HEM, neither of which has the slightest connection with the word ANTHEM. To take another word of seven letters, HERRING, we find this made up of HER and RING, neither word having any connection with HERRING.

In the following tests we start off with easy word combinations and get harder as we progress. All the words are put together in the same way and each small word is defined as shown in this typical example:

Corpulent + Feminine pronoun

FAT **HER** **FATHER**

You will find these double words fun to do even though a few of the words may be difficult to get. The par score is given in each case. The tests are graded according to their difficulty: A is easy, B is average, C is difficult and D is very difficult.

121. DUO-WORD TEST—A

Here are twenty six-letter words made up of two three-letter words each. These two words are defined in each case. Par for this test is 14 correct in four minutes.

1. Male adults + highest card in pack — — — — — —
2. Large body of water + male child — — — — — —
3. Opposite of ON + frozen water — — — — — —
4. One terminal + organ of hearing — — — — — —
5. Mischievous child + atmosphere — — — — — —
6. Army bed + heavy weight — — — — — —
7. Headgear + a color — — — — — —
8. Decay + past tense of eat — — — — — —
9. To ask for charity + unity — — — — — —
10. Spanish nobleman + locking device — — — — — —
11. A chum + a hero in aviation — — — — — —
12. To deface + alcoholic drink — — — — — —
13. By reason of + conscious self — — — — — —
14. Water barrier + writing instrument — — — — — —
15. Our nearest star + devoid of moisture — — — — — —
16. Distant + noisy quarrel — — — — — —
17. To succeed in competition + endeavor — — — — — —
18. A kind of tree + rock containing iron — — — — — —
19. A dog + not many — — — — — —
20. A venomous snake + anger — — — — — —

122. DUO-WORD TEST—B

Here are twenty six-letter words made up of two three-letter words each. These two words are defined in each case. Par for this test is 12 correct in five minutes.

1. Automobile + house dog — — — — — —
2. To stitch a garment + your time of life — — — — — —
3. Vehicle + decay — — — — — —
4. Meat of pig + allow — — — — — —
5. Large + a girl's name — — — — — —
6. Part of a dog + a man's name — — — — — —
7. To pretend + electrified particle — — — — — —
8. To join + past tense of lead — — — — — —
9. To move in fixed direction + golf term — — — — — —
10. Feminine pronoun + it's used in baseball — — — — — —
11. Part of a fish + a kind of beer — — — — — —
12. A number of two digits + to put on — — — — — —
13. Armed conflict + home of a lion — — — — — —
14. To place + to free — — — — — —
15. The legal profession + bottom of river — — — — — —
16. Amusement + man's name — — — — — —
17. Kitchen utensil + burned residue — — — — — —
18. Part of the body + terminal — — — — — —
19. To perceive + definite article — — — — — —

20. Dumb animal + to be affected by unknown illness — — — — — —

123. DUO-WORD TEST—C

Here are twenty six-letter words made up of two three-letter words each. These two words are defined in each case. Par for this test is 12 correct in ten minutes.

1. Water barrier + to demand; to question — — — — — —
2. Vital to the propagation of race + a heavy weight — — — — — —
3. Old piece of cloth + a preposition — — — — — —
4. A small young dog + what most of them are (singular) — — — — — —
5. A day of the week (abbr.) + vessel for holding ashes — — — — — —
6. A wager + a single beam of light — — — — — —
7. Golf term + definite article — — — — — —
8. Encountered + important to a bricklayer — — — — — —
9. To put on or dress in + past tense of eat — — — — — —
10. Undeveloped shoot + obtain — — — — — —
11. Small insect + alcoholic liquor — — — — — —
12. Parity + a helper — — — — — —
13. Feminine pronoun + long wide street (abbr.) — — — — — —

14. A prickly covering + French for water — — — — — —
15. A sailor + allow — — — — — —
16. A young swine + period of geological time — — — — — —
17. A small speck + period of one's life — — — — — —
18. The middle part + to come by — — — — — —
19. A hated rodent + feminine pronoun — — — — — —
20. A chum + a covering to a box — — — — — —

124. DUO-WORD TEST—D

This is a tough test to be done just the same as the three preceding ones. Par for this is 5 correct in fifteen minutes.

1. Mechanical lifter + yellow matter from suppuration — — — — — —
2. Coal distillation product + term in trigonometry (abbr.) — — — — — —
3. Lithuanian gold monetary unit + one picked from many — — — — — —
4. Feminine pronoun + period of geological time — — — — — —
5. A considerable quantity + electrical term — — — — — —
6. To gain or conquer + the very present — — — — — —
7. Commercial (abbr.) + man's name — — — — — —

8. To know how + girl's name — — — — — — —
9. A star + to be "in the know" — — — — — — —
10. Fly larva that infests the horse + a male cat — — — — — — —

125. DUO-WORD TEST—E

Here are twenty seven-letter words made up of one three-letter word and one four-letter word. Par for this is 14 correct in five minutes.

1. Grain of Iowa + frozen water — — — — — — —
2. Ostrichlike animal + tardy — — — — — — —
3. To tap gently + uproar — — — — — — —
4. Organ of hearing + most birds' homes — — — — — — —
5. Masculine pronoun + party in England — — — — — — —
6. Hawaiian wreath + positive — — — — — — —
7. A kind of sailing vessel + a fruity drink — — — — — — —
8. A transgression + a monarch — — — — — — —
9. Part of a book + a small insect — — — — — — —
10. Humane + a color — — — — — — —
11. A man-made slope + skill; dexterity — — — — — — —
12. A form of energy + barnyard fowl — — — — — — —

13. Equivalence + a short, quick cut with scissors — — — — — — —
14. Head gear + dimensions — — — — — — —
15. Listen to + a number — — — — — — —
16. By reason of + melody — — — — — — —
17. Part of the verb "to do" + consanguinity — — — — — — —
18. To cover; excel + Oriental grain — — — — — — —
19. Imaginary evil spirit + any special instruction — — — — — — —
20. Restore to health + pertaining to thee — — — — — — —

126. DUO-WORD TEST—F

This test is done in the same way as Test 5 and par is the same as for that test.

1. To obstruct + to win — — — — — — — —
2. Part of a circle + home of bees (plural) — — — — — — — —
3. Hinder + framework on which articles are displayed — — — — — — — —
4. Obliged; compelled + a steady pain — — — — — — — —

5. A round, flat object + above — — — — — — — —
6. To dress in one's best + an anesthetic — — — — — — — —
7. Writing instrument + a religious song — — — — — — — —
8. Except + a lock of human hair — — — — — — — —
9. Large room devoted to concerts + was in debt — — — — — — — —
10. A lair + a small weight — — — — — — — —
11. Remote; distant + •any object — — — — — — — —
12. Very young child + to unite or form a connection — — — — — — — —
13. Male adults + score sheet — — — — — — — —
14. Extend over + monarch — — — — — — — —
15. Method; way + reckon the value of — — — — — — — —
16. Time gone by + word of mouth — — — — — — — —
17. A New England state (abbr.) + measure of area — — — — — — — —
18. Coarse outer coat of wheat + a china vessel — — — — — — — —
19. By reason of + a natural fat (chemical) — — — — — — — —
20. Mischievous child + the numeral 1 — — — — — — — —

127. DUO-WORD TEST—G

Fill in the blanks to make twelve words of nine or ten letters. Here is an example:

Alcoholic drink + within + tiny insects = RUM + IN + ANTS = RUMINANTS

Par for this test is 8 correct in ten minutes.

1. Cylindrical metal container + past tense of do + past tense of eat

   — — — — — — — — —

2. Part of locomotive + part of the body + a male sheep

   — — — — — — — — —

3. A street vehicle + writing instrument + to endeavor

   — — — — — — — — —

4. Parity + the whole + elevated railroads (abbr.)

   — — — — — — — — —

5. Corpulent + feminine pronoun + flexible covering for the head

   — — — — — — — — — —

6. A chum + a fruit seed + past tense of eat

   — — — — — — — — —

7. A very large body of water + male child + having ability

   — — — — — — — — — —

8. In no manner or to no extent + frozen water + having ability

— — — — — — — — — —

9. A false pretense; a sham + young male child + small insect

— — — — — — — — — —

10. Parity + male child + period of one's life

— — — — — — — — —

11. Part of a circumference + strike + to act in a frenzy

— — — — — — — — — —

12. Unnecessary activity; bustle + a hated rodent + electrical term

— — — — — — — — —

128. FILL-IN PUZZLES

The following fill-in puzzles are unique. If you get one word you have all the other words because all words in each diagram contain the same letters arranged differently. Here is an example:

```
        T
—   —   —
T
—   —   —
        T
—   —   —
```

You are given the letter T in this three-letter word and it is for you to find the other two letters. It shouldn't take you more than two minutes to see that those letters are A and R and the filled-in puzzle is:

A R T
T A R
R A T

The par time is given for each puzzle. See if you can better it.

a.
_ _ E
_ E _
E _ _
(*2 minutes*)

b.
_ _ P
_ P _
P _ _
(*5 minutes*)

c.
R _ _
_ R _
_ _ R
(*2 minutes*)

d.
T _ _ _
_ T _ _
_ _ T _
_ _ _ T
(*3 minutes*)

e.
S _ _ _
_ S _ _
_ _ S _
_ _ _ S
(*5 minutes*)

f.
_ O _ _
_ _ O _
_ O _ _
_ _ O _
_ O _ _
O _ _ _
(*4 minutes*)

g.

			E	S
			R	E
			E	S
			R	E
			E	S

(*6 minutes*)

h.

			E	S
			R	E
			E	R
			R	S
			E	S

(*6 minutes*)

i,

		A	M	
	A	M		
M	A			
M		A		
			A	M

(*4 minutes*)

j.

P	R				
	P	R			
		P	R		
R		P			
	R		P		
		R		P	

(*7 minutes*)

k.

	I	T			S
T	I				S
S		I	T		
			I	T	S
			I	T	S
	I	S	T		

(*10 minutes*)

TRIPLE-WORD PUZZLES

Here are thirty-two *brand-new* word puzzles, new in both principle and design, that have never appeared in any book or magazine before. If you follow the directions we think you will find them a lot of fun to do.

Fill in the dashes first and pay no attention to the boxes —they are to be filled in later on. The dashes, of course, are letters in words which are defined to the right of the dashed lines. All words are of six letters, but the words you are to find first are of *five letters* each. After finding each *five-letter word* merely fill in the box to make an entirely new and different word of *six* letters. If you do this correctly the six letters in the boxes, reading from upper left to lower right, will spell a word. Here is an example:

[E] S T A T E

S [L] A V E S

G R [A] I N S

M I S [T] E R

G R I P [E] S

C L O S E [D]

Note that the five-letter words are independent of the letters in the boxes and each letter in a box makes a new six-letter word, viz., ESTATE from STATE; SLAVES from SAVES, etc. Note also that the word in the boxes spells ELATED. Now go to work on the following.

129-30. AMERICAN CITIES

The letters in the boxes spell the names of two American cities.

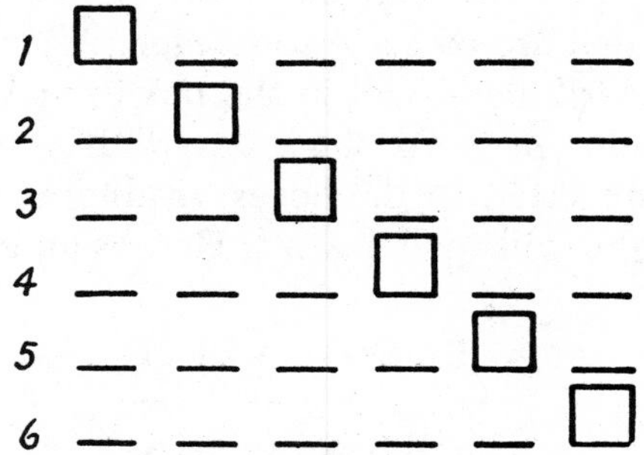

Definitions:

1. Radiant energy which produces sight.
2. A metric liquid measure.
3. Mother.
4. A puzzling problem.
5. A metric measure of length.
6. To place underground.

Definitions:

1. Wrath.
2. A refuge; shelter.
3. Hinged barriers.
4. Restored to health again.
5. The male of a red deer.
6. An appetizing dressing for food.

131-2. COMMON FLOWERS

The letters in the boxes spell the names of two common flowers.

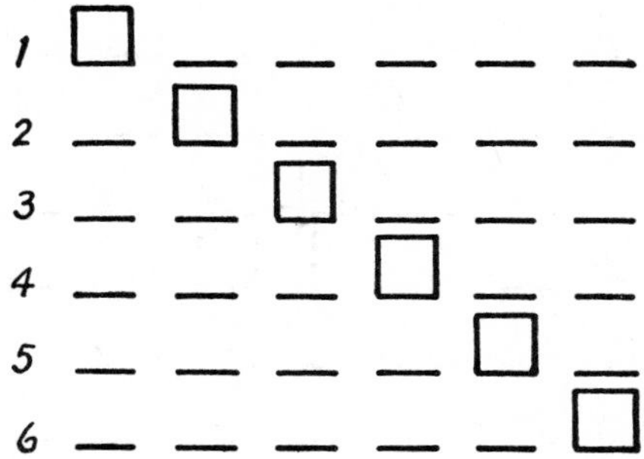

Definitions:

1. Female relatives.
2. Lays plans; conspires.
3. Propelled a boat with a pole.
4. A clearing in an English moor
5. Bony fish (plural).
6. A perfectly flat surface.

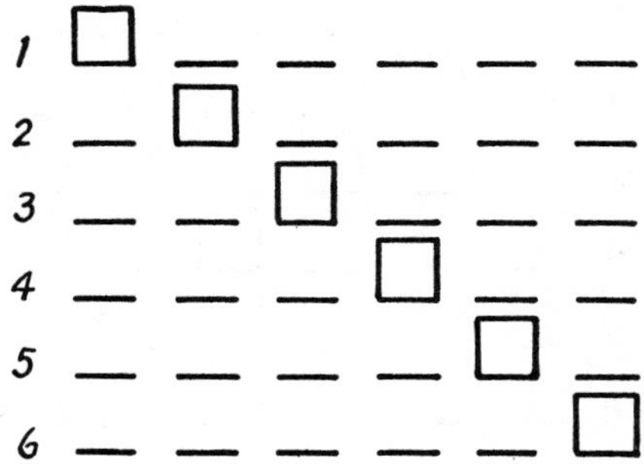

Definitions:

1. Inclines toward.
2. Plunges head foremost.
3. Lowlands.
4. Removed ore from the earth.
5. A condition of being.
6. Depart.

133-4. WINES

The letters in the boxes spell the names of two common wines.

1 □ _ _ _ _ _
2 _ □ _ _ _ _
3 _ _ □ _ _ _
4 _ _ _ □ _ _
5 _ _ _ _ □ _
6 _ _ _ _ _ □

Definitions:

1. They grow on the head.
2. That which is eaten or drunk (plural).
3. Smiles broadly.
4. Definite localities.
5. Front parts of the legs.
6. An article of furniture.

1 □ _ _ _ _ _
2 _ □ _ _ _ _
3 _ _ □ _ _ _
4 _ _ _ □ _ _
5 _ _ _ _ □ _
6 _ _ _ _ _ □

Definitions:

1. Borrows money on personal property.
2. Wooden containers.
3. Discovers; chances upon.
4. Applies heat.
5. To measure; to serve as a standard of measurement.
6. Lineage; family.

135-6. POPULAR CARD GAMES

The letters in the boxes spell the names of two popular card games.

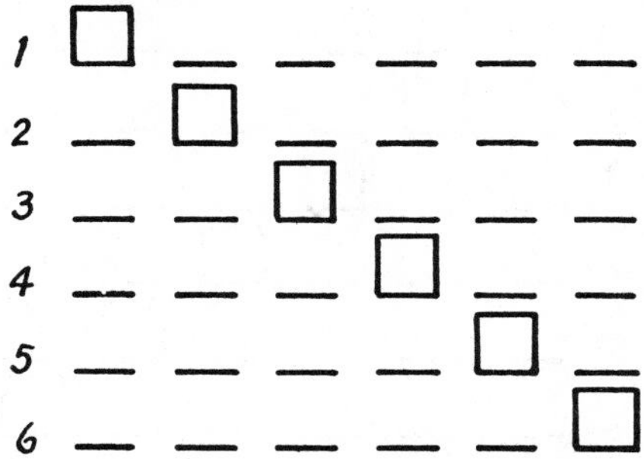

Definitions:

1. A light weight.
2. A number of collections of tents.
3. Trousers.
4. More insolent.
5. Makes thinner.
6. A fight or quarrel.

Definitions:

1. A small animal beginning with O.
2. Poets of old.
3. Calls for as a price in exchange.
4. A portion of something.
5. Distant suns.
6. To depart.

137-8. METALS

The letters in the boxes spell the names of two metals.

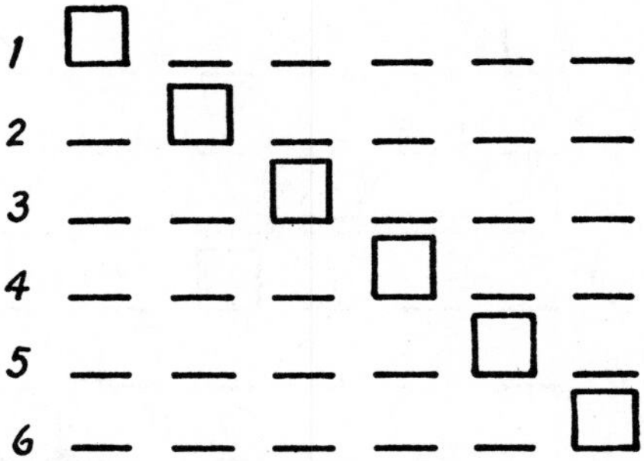

Definitions:

1. Lighting devices.
2. Small liquid measures.
3. Acts of selling.
4. The slender growths that support the flowers.
5. Part of an ox's stomach.
6. Near by.

Definitions:

1. Opposite of late.
2. Babble; foolishly loquacious.
3. A small speculator.
4. Those who watch secretly.
5. Architectural floor layouts.
6. Push.

139-40. ANIMALS

The letters in the boxes spell the names of two animals.

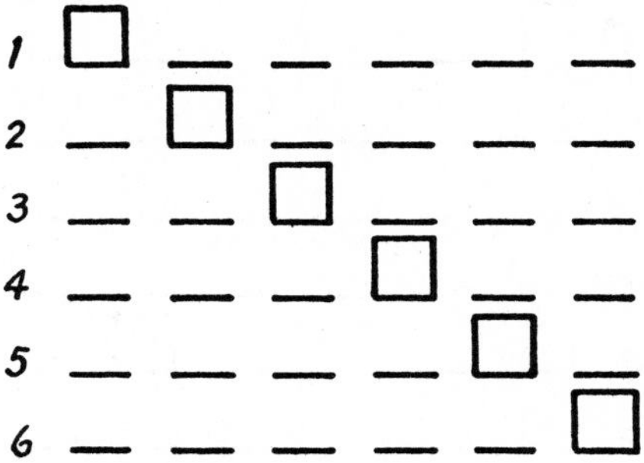

Definitions:

1. Different from the one specified.
2. Tool-making machine.
3. A car devoted to serving meals.
4. One who laces.
5. Dishwater and other dirty waters.
6. What wasps do.

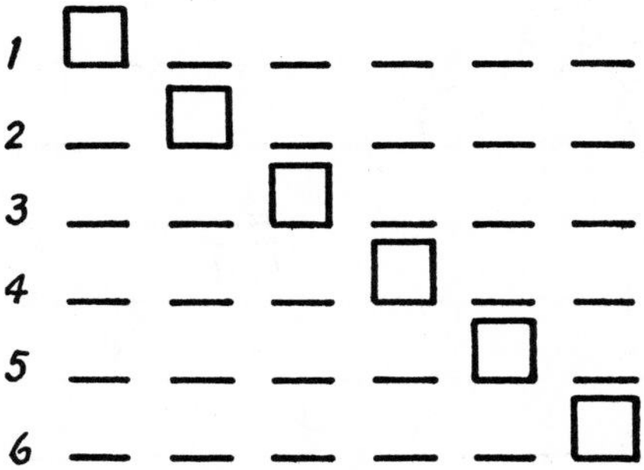

Definitions:

1. Competitions of speed.
2. Light midday meal.
3. Strips off.
4. Continuous metal-bearing veins.
5. Photostats (abbr.).
6. To burn the tips of, as hair.

141-2. VEGETABLES

The letters in the boxes spell the names of two vegetables.

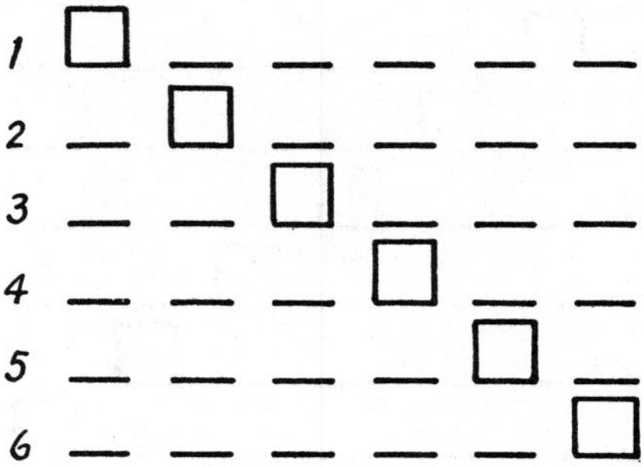

Definitions:

1. Delicate networks of threads.
2. Poets of old.
3. One who bites.
4. A disease peculiar to dogs.
5. Dumb animals, also very stupid persons.
6. Western farm.

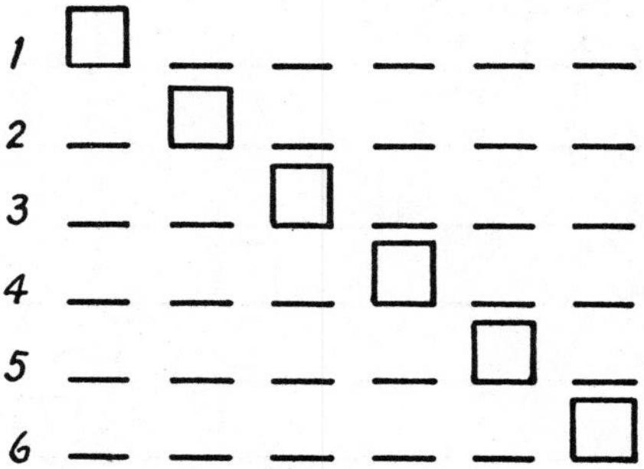

Definitions:

1. Speed; dispatch; hurry.
2. Hard skeleton of tiny marine zoophytes.
3. Male cooks.
4. Furnished with the sole of a shoe.
5. Long, thin, horizontal wooden strips.
6. Worries; troubles.

143-4. RIVERS

The letters in the boxes spell the names of two famous rivers.

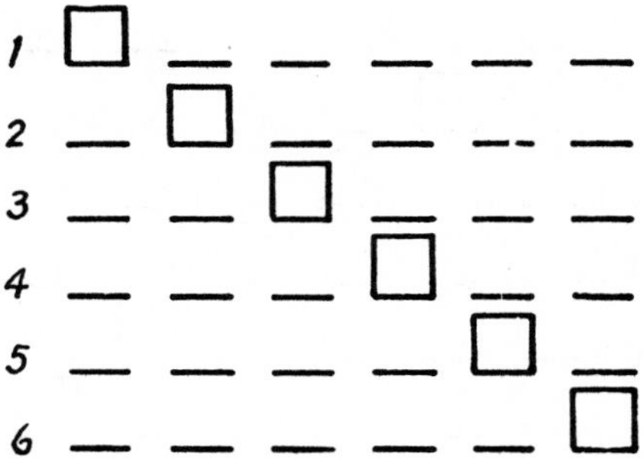

Definitions:

1. Circular.
2. Offers for sale.
3. Singing festivals.
4. Forced open with a crow-bar.
5. A small hall for display of art.
6. Mathematical relation of one quantity to another.

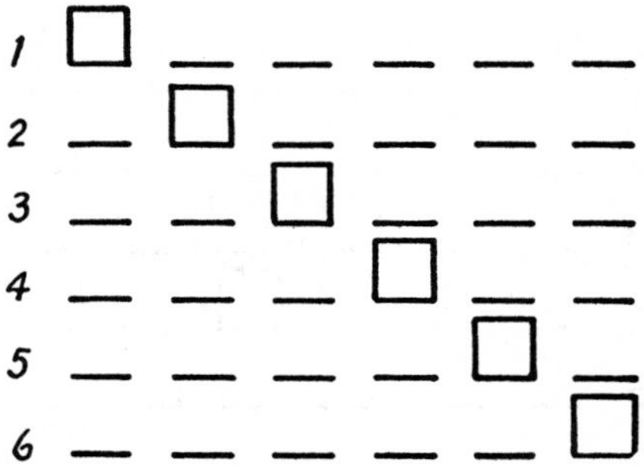

Definitions:

1. Change.
2. Backbone.
3. What we all have three times a day.
4. What all plants have.
5. Rooms furnished for bathing.
6. Girl's name.

145-6. BOY'S NAMES

The letters in the boxes spell the names of two boys.

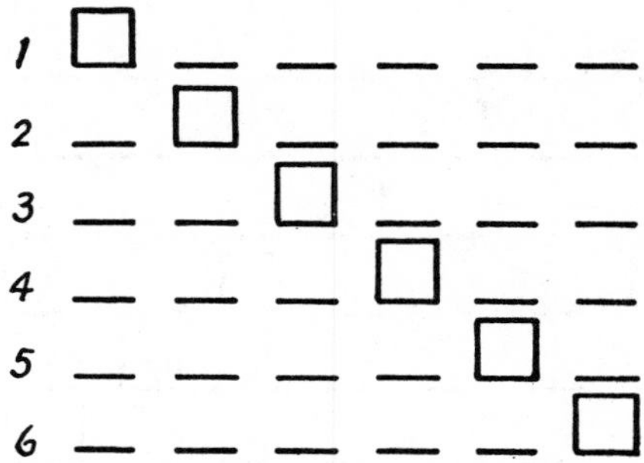

Definitions:

1. A gaseous element.
2. Weighed down; burdened with.
3. An unwanted mark from paint or grease.
4. Noisy discharges fired from revolvers.
5. Rabbits.
6. Any long, narrow and thin piece.

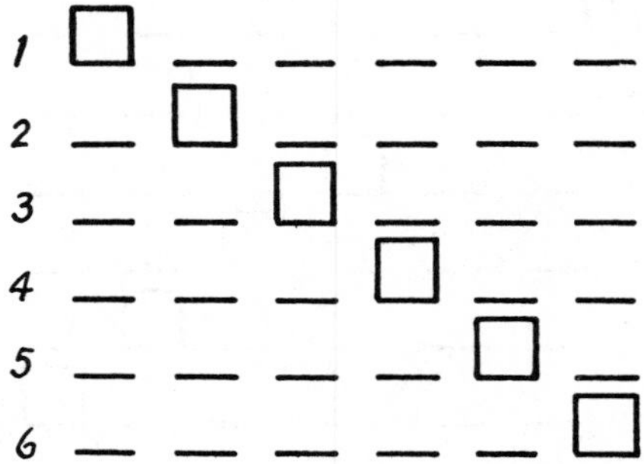

Definitions:

1. Musical instruments.
2. Weeds out; sorts out.
3. Ceases movement.
4. Devices set to catch mice.
5. To drive away; to shun.
6. Bright; intelligent.

147-8. GIRL'S NAMES

The letters in the boxes spell the names of two girls.

Definitions:

1. A flower.
2. Tropical trees.
3. Tracts of marshy waste-lands.
4. At a subsequent time.
5. A young shrub or tree.
6. The state of being bright and lustrous.

Definitions:

1. It is shot from a bow.
2. Part of a fireplace.
3. These are used to water the flowers.
4. Sat for a photograph or portrait.
5. Horses used to do this at "horseless carriages."
6. Break off relations with.

149-50. MUSICAL INSTRUMENTS

The letters in the boxes spell the names of two musical instruments.

1 □ ___ ___ ___ ___ ___
2 ___ □ ___ ___ ___ ___
3 ___ ___ □ ___ ___ ___
4 ___ ___ ___ □ ___ ___
5 ___ ___ ___ ___ □ ___
6 ___ ___ ___ ___ ___ □

Definitions:

1. A narrow passageway or street.
2. To hurl out suddenly.
3. Trades one article for another.
4. Unsophisticated country men.
5. A long-legged wading bird.
6. A division of an extended poem.

1 □ ___ ___ ___ ___ ___
2 ___ □ ___ ___ ___ ___
3 ___ ___ □ ___ ___ ___
4 ___ ___ ___ □ ___ ___
5 ___ ___ ___ ___ □ ___
6 ___ ___ ___ ___ ___ □

Definitions:

1. A bar suspended on a fulcrum.
2. A type of jazz music.
3. Caverns in rocks.
4. Equivalent given in exchange; amount to be paid.
5. Clips off with a pair of scissors.
6. Backbone.

151-2. BIRDS

The letters in the boxes spell the names of two common birds.

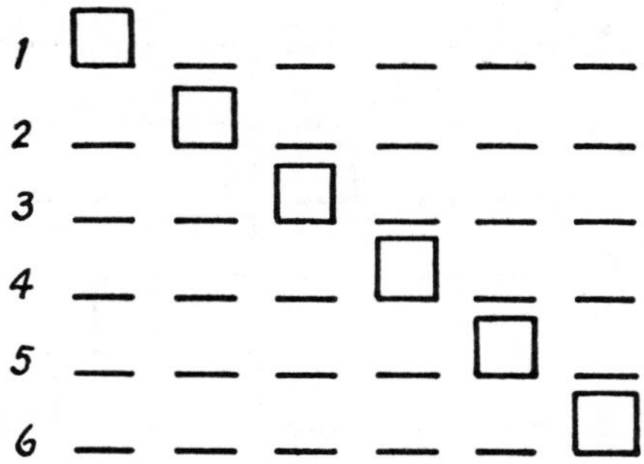

Definitions:

1. A kind of artificial silk.
2. Faint hues of color.
3. Grandma did this with corsets and shoes.
4. An open fireplace for heating metals.
5. What the sun does every morning.
6. The place of a person as occupied by a successor.

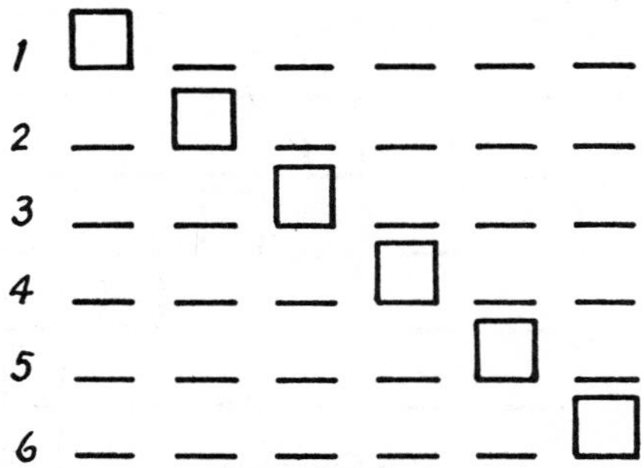

Definitions:

1. Made a request for.
2. Telling untruths.
3. Rows of boxes in an opera house.
4. Not fresh any more.
5. A sudden, extreme effort (usually spelled with u).
6. Royal.

153-4. STATES

The letters in the boxes spell the names of two states.

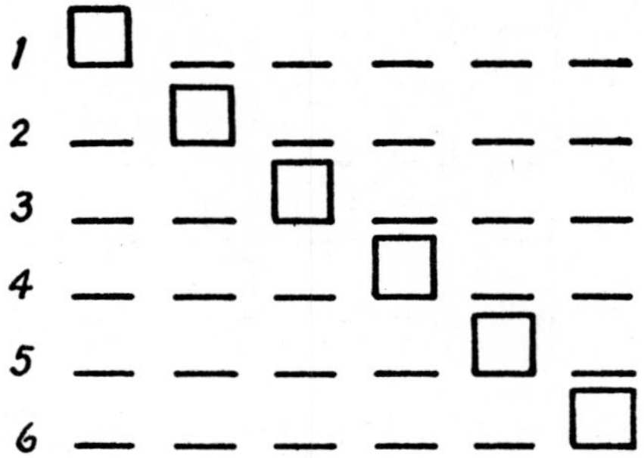

Definitions:

1. Dwells or resides.
2. Small, mean and miserly.
3. What Junior does before exams.
4. Long, narrow straps used to drive a horse.
5. Narrow foot roads through fields.
6. Depart.

Definitions:

1. Between sunrise and sunset.
2. A shallow, circular dish.
3. Fits of anger.
4. Rests in expectation.
5. An ocean steamer.
6. Pertaining to battleships.

155-6. WEARING APPAREL

The letters in the boxes spell the names of two articles of wearing apparel.

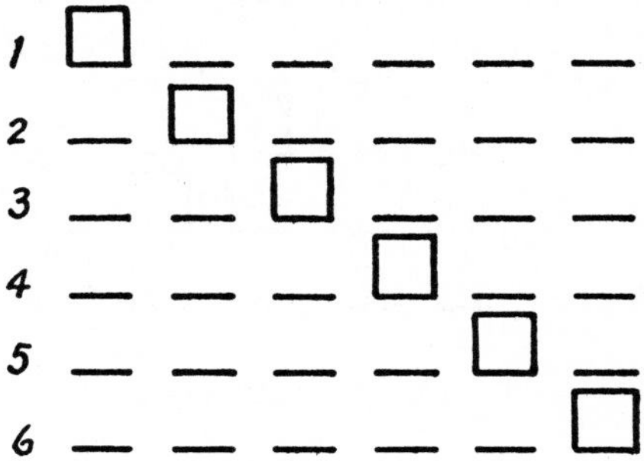

Definitions:

1. To fish with hook and line.
2. Abstains from eating.
3. Part of a ridged roof.
4. Removed by cutting.
5. Fakes.
6. To move with a rapid, sweeping stroke.

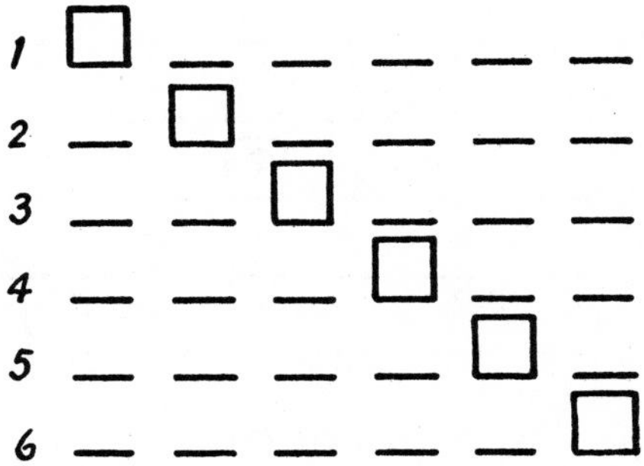

Definitions:

1. Parts of a tree.
2. Stop.
3. A domestic animal.
4. Financial transactions.
5. A midshipman.
6. A tiny fly.

157-8. MISCELLANEOUS WORDS

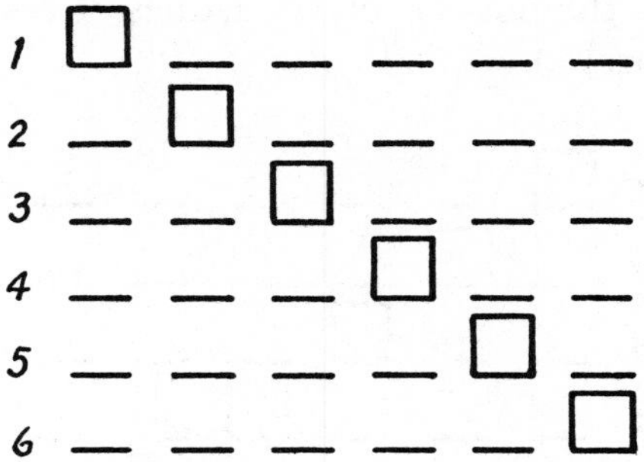

Definitions:

1. Great numbers of persons or things.
2. Any animal except man.
3. Challenged.
4. Less coarse.
5. A girl who is just married.
6. Pertaining to humanity.

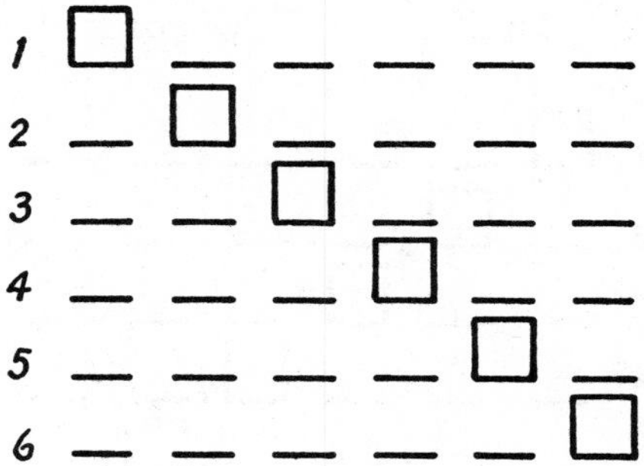

Definitions:

1. To permit.
2. An anesthetic.
3. Found agreeable.
4. Old-fashioned name for a high hat.
5. Distant suns.
6. Article of furniture.

159. NO DUPLICATES

Here are 10 of the longest familiar words in the English language which contain *no duplication of letters.* You are given four of the letters correctly placed in each word and it is for you to complete all the words in twelve minutes. Can you do it?

1. P___G___ND_
2. __M_A__I__R
3. _O___AN__I_
4. _W__C_B__R_
5. R_____IZ___Y
6. _T_N___A__I_
7. B___R____I_S
8. _UB__D__A____
9. R__U_L___N_
10. _U_BW____R_

160. AUTOMOTIVE WORDS

Here are thirty five-letter words that are familiar to everyone who drives a car. Eleven of these thirty words are to be filled in in the blanks below in such a way that all the center letters, reading vertically down, will spell an eleven-letter word which is very important to every automobile. How quickly can you do this? Par is 7 minutes. The second letter of each word has already been filled in so it is up to you to complete the words which are included among the thirty following:

AXLES	DRIVE	GAUGE	PANEL	SPARK
BOLTS	DOORS	LIGHT	PEDAL	SHAFT
BRAKE	DISCS	LAMPS	PLUGS	TIRES
BULBS	FLOAT	LOCKS	RADIO	TUBES
CHOKE	FRAME	METER	SHIFT	VALVE
CRANK	GEARS	MOTOR	SPOKE	WHEEL

1. _ A _ _ _
2. _ A _ _ _
3. _ U _ _ _
4. _ I _ _ _
5. _ R _ _ _
6. _ O _ _ _
7. _ H _ _ _
8. _ O _ _ _
9. _ H _ _ _
10. _ L _ _ _
11. _ A _ _ _

161. WEIGHTED WORDS

The reason for this title will not be apparent until after you solve the puzzle. However, you can see that each of the letter combinations below needs the added weight of a letter on each end, to make it good English. Of course there are many initial and terminal letters that might be used to make five-letter words with these three in the middle. But you are to find initial and terminal letters that form an acrostic when read downwards. Can you do it?

_ L U M _
_ X T R _
_ E B E _
_ L O R _
_ L F I _
_ O M I _
_ A B L _

162. A NATIONAL HOLIDAY AND WHAT IT CELEBRATES

The first letter of each word, reading down, gives the name of a national holiday and the final letter of each word, reading down, will give the name of what it celebrates. The definitions are not given in any special order. How quickly can you fill these in? Par is 17 minutes.

_ _ _ _ _
_ _ _ _ _
_ _ _ _ _
_ _ _ _ _
_ _ _ _ _
_ _ _ _ _
_ _ _ _ _
_ _ _ _ _
_ _ _ _ _
_ _ _ _ _
_ _ _ _ _
_ _ _ _ _

Definitions:

A musical wind instrument. Liquid from a fruit. A fake, a sham. A flower grown mostly in Holland. Molds, mildews. Reversed the process of doing. The open sea. A gun. Pertaining to the city. A residence. Verse of songlike form. Contraction for you are.

163. A MONTH AND WHAT OCCURS IN IT

The first letters of each word, reading down, spell the name of a month in the fall and the last letters, reading down, spell the name of an event that occurs in the month. The definitions are given in no special order. How quickly can you fill these in? Par is 10 minutes.

— — — — — —
— — — — — —
— — — — — —
— — — — — —
— — — — — —
— — — — — —
— — — — — —
— — — — — —

Definitions:

Decayed. A place where food is bought. Amorous; pertaining to love. Agile. A bag carried by a traveler. The rudimentary form of anything in its earliest development. An expression equivalent to "Long live the Emperor!" A trying experience.

164. A CERTAIN TREE AND A GREAT GENERAL

The first letters of each word, reading down, spell the name of a certain kind of tree—its full name—and the last letters, reading down, spell the name of a great general who is associated with that tree. The definitions are not given in any special order. How quickly can you fill these in? Par is 20 minutes.

— — — — — —
— — — — — —
— — — — — —
— — — — — —
— — — — — —
— — — — — —
— — — — — —
— — — — — —
— — — — — —
— — — — — —

Definitions:

Something appetizing. A naval officer. A petty naval officer doing clerical work. The gold unit of Portugal. Immature; youthful. Goes inside. Making an effort. Laughing animal. Cylindrical tube propelled by exploding gas. Native Indian language of Guadeloupe.

165. A SCIENTIFIC PRINCIPLE AND ITS DISCOVERER

The first letter of each word, reading down, will give the name of a well-known scientific principle and the last letters, reading down, will give the name of the discoverer of that principle. The definitions are not in order. Par is 20 minutes.

— — — — —
— — — — —
— — — — —
— — — — —
— — — — —
— — — — —
— — — — —
— — — — —
— — — — —
— — — — —

Definitions:

A measure of liquid volume. An ancient fruit. Pertaining to the eye. What birds build. The power of discerning fitness. Famous work of Homer. Plants in general; plant life. To put to shame. Opposite the middle of a ship's side. The total tonal effect produced by an orchestra.

166. A FAMOUS CITY AND WHAT IT IS FAMOUS FOR

The final letters of each word, reading down, spell the name of a famous Western city and the first letters, reading down, spell the name of what that city is famous for. The definitions are not in any special order. How quickly can you fill these in? Par is 15 minutes.

— — — — —
— — — — —
— — — — —
— — — — —
— — — — —
— — — — —
— — — — —
— — — — —
— — — — —
— — — — —

Definitions:

To go one better. Having partaken of a meal. To clean with water. Pieces of vocal music. Ethical. A country in Asia. A long bandage used for a broken arm. To gauge by means of the tongue. Depravities. To take advantage of.

167. A NATURAL LAW AND ITS DISCOVERER

The first letter of each word, reading down, will give the name of a famous natural law and the last letters, reading down, will give the name of the discoverer of that law. The definitions are not in order. Be sure to fill in the entire puzzle. Par is 10 minutes.

— — — —
— — — —
— — — —
— — — —
— — — —
— — — —
— — — —

Definitions:

The present month (abbr.). Mongolian desert. Water from the clouds. Spindle on which a wheel turns. Three considered collectively. Range of sight. To open the mouth wide from being bored.

168. A FAMOUS ARTIST AND HIS MOST FAMOUS WORK

The first letter of each word, reading down, will give the name of a world-famous artist and the last letters, reading down, will give the name of the masterpiece for which he is so well known. The definitions are not in order. Par is 10 minutes.

— — — —
— — — —
— — — —
— — — —
— — — —
— — — —
— — — —
— — — —

Definitions:

The end of every prayer. Part of a passport. To come into sight; to appear above the surface. Outlawed terrorist party of Germany. Part of a pedestal. Small covering for the head (plural). A mental concept. An image of a divinity.

169. A FAMOUS AMERICAN STATESMAN AND WHAT HE IS KNOWN FOR

The first letter of each word, reading down, will give the name of a famous American statesman and the last letters, reading down, will give one of the most important words in our language which will always be associated with this statesman. The definitions are not in order. Par is 10 minutes.

— — — — — —
— — — — — —
— — — — — —
— — — — — —
— — — — — —
— — — — — —
— — — — — —
— — — — — —
— — — — — —

Definitions:

A measure of depth. Not anyone. Liquid of the mouth. To be criticized. A naturalist who works in a national park. Unusual. Pertaining to an acid of potassium oxalate. Circumstances of life. The art of painting on wet plaster before it dries.

170. A GREAT AMERICAN STATESMAN AND WHAT HE ABOLISHED

The final letter of each word, reading down, gives the name of a beloved ex-President of the United States and the first letters of each word, reading down, will give the evil that he abolished. The definitions are not in order. Par is 15 minutes.

— — — — — — —
— — — — — — —
— — — — — — —
— — — — — — —
— — — — — — —
— — — — — — —
— — — — — — —

Definitions:

Enough to fill a room. Stony particles ejected from a volcano. A highwayman. Prohibition of shipping to other ports. A drug for headaches. A sea bird with large wings. Pertaining to hunting.

171. A FAMOUS COMPOSER AND HIS FAMOUS COMPOSITION

The first letter of each word, reading down, will give the name of a world-renowned composer and the last letters, reading down, will give the name of one of his most famous compositions. The definitions are not in order. Par is 10 minutes.

— — — — — —
— — — — — —
— — — — — —
— — — — — —
— — — — — —
— — — — —
— — — — — —
— — — — — —
— — — — — —

Definitions:

Noisy confusion. Next after seventh. A kind of candy containing nuts. A young organism in the early stages of development. A place of lodging; an inn. A gold coin of Portugal. The act of casting a ballot. Paper placed in a printing press between the impression surface and the paper to be printed. A giraffe-like animal of the Congo.

WORD DESIGNS

The following word-design puzzles are somewhat like crosswords with the actual letters forming the various designs instead of black squares. In most cases only the first and last letters of the words spell words vertically and in every case words are formed horizontally. The letters that appear in the diagrams never appear in the filled-in words in any other position. If, for example, a word-design puzzle shows a number of E's forming the design, there are no *other* E's in that puzzle The same is true of other letters. The definitions are given in regular order, the top word being No. 1, the second word No. 2 and so on, all the way down. All words are in *Webster's New International Dictionary*. This section is intended for the solo player who should not require more than ten minutes for any one puzzle.

172

The first and last letters spell words vertically; all others are five-letter words horizontally.

S		L		S
		E		
L	E		E	L
		E		
S		L		S

Definitions:

1. Fibres obtained from the silk worm (plural)
2. The scene of any contest
3. Flat
4. A burglary; larceny
5. Musical compositions for one singer or player

173

The first and last letters spell words vertically; all others are five-letter words horizontally.

S				S
		A		
	A	S	A	
		A		
S				S

Definitions:

1. Causes to go
2. Egg-shaped
3. Pertaining to the nose
4. Cup used by Jesus at the Last Supper
5. The impoverished parts of a city

174

The first and last letters spell words vertically; all others are five-letter words horizontally.

E				E
	E		E	
		E		
	E		E	
E				E

Definitions:

1. The best class of people
2. A bar on a fulcrum used for lifting
3. Another name for hives
4. Taken out; omitted
5. Large bird, a symbol of the United States

175

The first and last letters spell words vertically; all others are five-letter words horizontally.

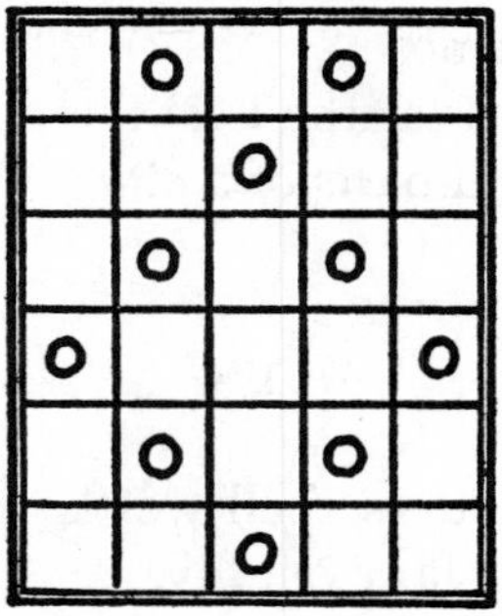

Definitions:

1. Musical compositions for one singer or player
2. A small town or village; a hamlet
3. A rotating member of a machine
4. To do better than
5. An armadillo
6. To talk in a very loud voice; to yell

176

The first and last letters spell words vertically; all others are five-letter words horizontally.

E				E
		E		
	E		E	
E				E
	E		E	
		E		

Definitions:

1. To avoid by clever means
2. A length of yarn wound in a coil
3. Any doctrine or principle held as true
4. A large bird, a symbol of the United States
5. To direct the attention or thoughts of
6. Throws off readily

177

All words here are horizontal. There are no A's other than those shown.

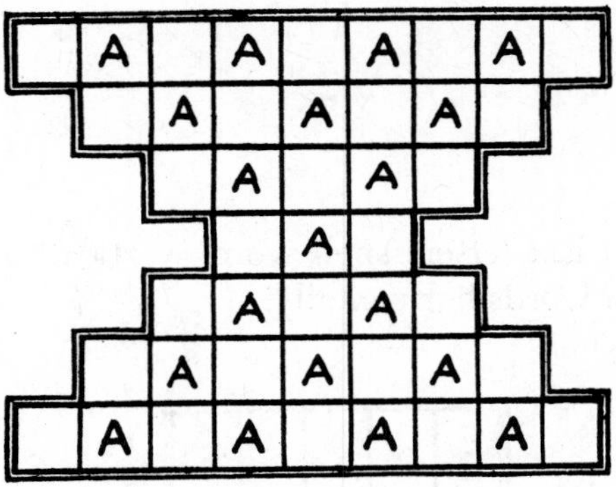

Definitions:

1. A kind of raft
2. A Southern pulpy fruit (plural)
3. Pertaining to the nose
4. Flying mammal
5. Resulting in death
6. A group of merchants traveling in the desert
7. Ruling prince in India

178

The first and last letters spell words vertically; all others are six-letter words horizontally.

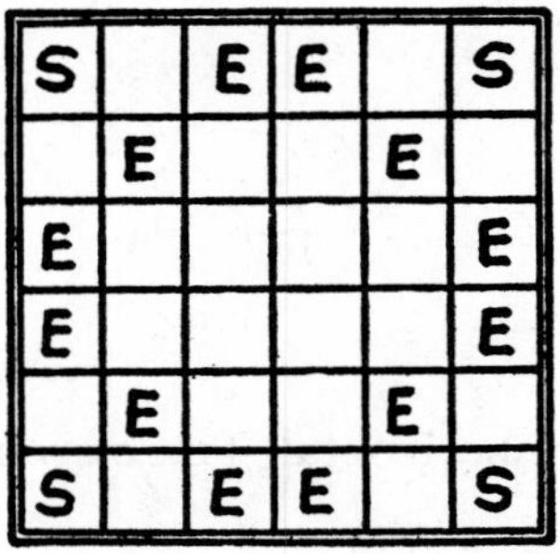

Definitions:

1. Reposes in unconsciousness overnight
2. The abode of God
3. Can be eaten; fit to eat
4. To tolerate
5. One who tears
6. Guides the course of

179

All words in this puzzle are seven-letter words horizontally.

G			T			G
		T		T		
	T				T	
T			G			T
	T				T	
		T		T		
G			T			G

Definitions:

1. Open latticework of wood or metal
2. Turned about the axis
3. Thoroughfares in a city
4. Touching as a straight line in relation to a circle, curve or surface
5. Surreptitious procedure
6. Properties
7. Satisfying fully; being a glutton.

180

The first and last letters spell words vertically; all others are six-letter words horizontally.

R	E			E	R
		R	R		
		R	R		
E					E
R	E			E	R

Definitions:

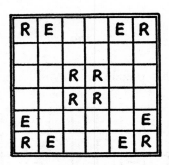

1. One who reads
2. Large tropical American lizard
3. A common vegetable
4. A common cheer; expression of joy
5. To render able
6. To make or cause to become

181

All words here are horizontal. There are no A's other than those shown.

S			A			S
		A		A		
	A		A		A	
A		A		A		A
	A		A		A	
		A		A		
S			A			S

Definitions:

1. Rectangles of equal sides
2. Parlor pantomime word game
3. A group of merchants traveling in the desert
4. A Southern State
5. Material used in building roads
6. Offensively noisy; obtrusive
7. Parts of yarn that make a rope

182

All words here are horizontal. There are no U's, N's or S's other than those shown.

S		U	N		S
	U			N	
U					N
U					N
	U			N	
S		U	N		S

Definitions:

1. Shoves or turns out of the way
2. An excursion or pleasure trip
3. The northern section of Manhattan Island
4. Poor boy of the streets
5. Sending forth fumes
6. Anything audible (plural)

183

All words here are horizontal. There are no L's or E's other than those shown.

L			E			L
	L				L	
		E		E		
E			L			E
		E		E		
	L				L	
L			E			L

Definitions:

1. Following the exact wording of
2. Pertaining to more than one
3. Place where beer is made
4. To place inside of
5. A gift
6. Suavely
7. Pertaining to the side

184

All words here are horizontal. There are no I's other than those shown.

			I			
		I		I		
	I				I	
I						I
	I				I	
		I		I		
			I			

Definitions:

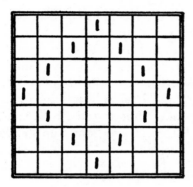

1. A limited amount; a moderate amount
2. A basis for brilliant dyes
3. A kind of bread in small, soft cake form
4. A combining form, from the Latin *insectum*
5. A circular journey
6. What the sun is always doing
7. The most or the greatest amount

185. WHEEL OF WORDS

Here is a wheel with sixteen spokes in it, each spoke representing a word. The words are alternately seven and five letters as you can see from the diagram. The seven-letter words either begin with the big S in the center or end with it according to the arrows. The five-letter words can begin with any letter but must end with the letter on the rim of the wheel. All words read as indicated by the arrows. The big sixteen-letter word which you see spelled all the way around the circle is INCOMPREHENSIBLE, reading clockwise. The letter T is in its correct position in all of the sixteen words so it is up to you to find words that fit all the requirements and fill in this diagram. Start at the top with the letter I. The first word, for example, is INTAKES and reads down. The next word is a five-letter word which must end in N and have a T for the third letter since it reads upwards according to the arrow. Continue until you have filled in the entire diagram. You should be able to do this in 15 minutes.

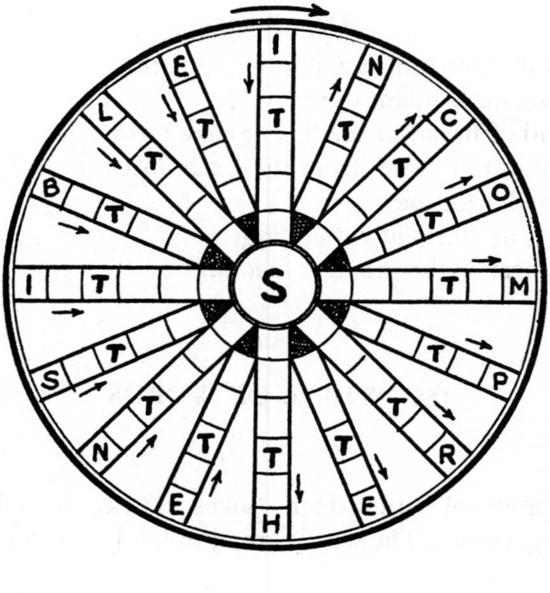

MATHEMATICAL PUZZLES

186. THE BARGAIN HUNTERS

A group of women bought a number of items at a bargain counter. All of the items sold for the same price and the total amount paid by all the women was $2.03, exclusive of the tax. If each item cost more than 10¢, how many women were in the group and what did each item cost?

187. FAMILY MATTERS

Both my son and I were born on the last day of February in years that are divisible by four. On February 28th, 1948, I celebrated my birthday and also the fact that I was three times my son's age. How old am I and how old is my son?

188. FAIR AND SQUARE

Yesterday I divided $12 equally among my children. The product of all the amounts that I gave to these children equals the number of square feet in a certain number of square yards. How many children have I and how much did each child receive?

189. MY YOUNG BROTHER

My young brother was born in a year which, when divided by two and turned upside down and divided by four, gives a number whose square root was my brother's age in 1929. How old was my brother in 1950?

190. JANE AND PETER

Jane and Peter are my two young children. Both are more than ten and less than twenty. The cube of Peter's age plus the square of Jane's age gives the year in which my wife was born. If I am five years older than my wife, what was the age of each member of my family in 1972?

191. TROUBLESOME FRACTION

Twice a fraction plus half that fraction times that fraction equals that fraction. What is the fraction?

192. WHAT A GIRL!

Dorothy lived in Eatontown, N. J., and made her boy friends work for their dates with her. She met a young man in 1946 who asked her for her phone number and here was her reply: "If you have enough brains to work out my phone number from the following information I'll be delighted to see you again and be your girl friend. I graduated from college a few years ago and my father was as old as I am now when I was born. Divide the year in which my father was born by eight and add it to the square root of a certain Presidential election year. Now add the result to the number of square inches in J square feet and you may call me at that number."
Assuming that Dorothy was extremely pretty and attractive and between the ages of twenty-two and twenty-eight, what number did you call to date her?
Hint: Rural phone numbers in 1946 usually contained three digits plus a letter.

193. IT'S FUN TO BE FOLD

A piece of typewriter paper 8½" x 11" is folded as shown in the diagram. As you can see, the angle that the top of the paper makes with the left margin is 45° and the projection A-B is 2⅞". What is the length of the fold C-D? (Correct to one-tenth of an inch.)

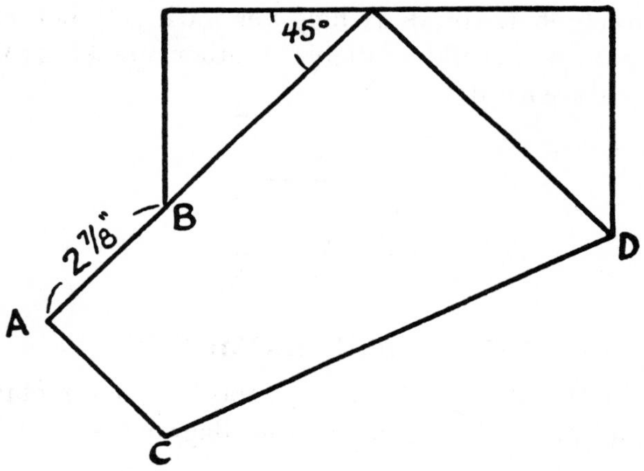

194. THREE GENERATIONS

My son's age is the same as my father's with the digits reversed. The product of their ages gives the year in which I was married. If I am twice as old as my son, how old am I, how old is my son, and how old is my father?

195. THE JUNKVILLE RAILROAD

A railroad runs straight from Punkton to Junkville. Mainfield is on this line just half way between Punkton and Junkville. Hotberg is just as far from Punkton as it is from Mainfield and Mainfield is as far from Hotberg as it is from Junkville. If it is twenty miles from Punkton to Hotberg, how far is Hotberg from Junkville?

196. PLEASE HELP ALICE

Poor little Alice started to do this multiplication problem but was spanked and sent to bed before she had a chance to complete it. If you don't help her she'll get another "z" in her arithmetic and probably another spanking. What can you do with it?

```
        .  .  7
        .  .  .
        -------
        .  .  9
  .  .  .
  -------------
  3  .  .  1  9
```

197. SIMPLE GEOMETRY

What are the areas of the narrow and the wide rectangles from the information given in the diagram?

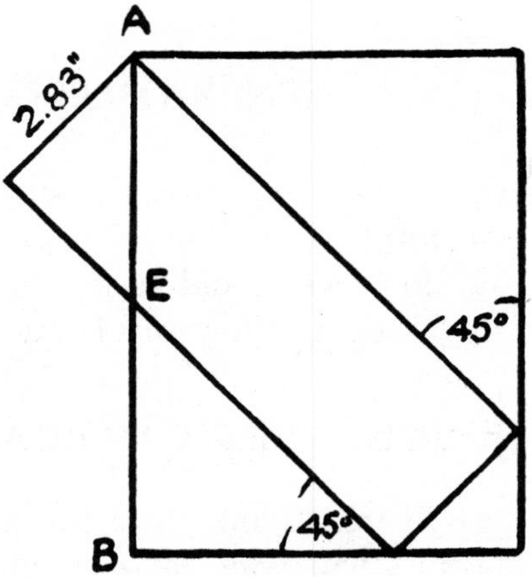

198. HIGH FINANCE

If I add five dollars to what I had before I spent five

dollars I find that I would have had five times as much as I have now. How much did I have originally?

199. JAPAN'S LOSSES

During the Second World War, General Nuisance, in an order of the day, issued the following statement:
"This was a bad day for Japan. The number of Japanese prisoners taken in the present drive can easily be found from the following simple addition:

```
  N I P S
  Q U I T
---------
Q U I C K
```

To help you along I'll tell you that S = 5, P = 4 and T = 3." How many prisoners did General Nuisance take?

200. THE CLEVER CARPENTER

A carpenter had to construct a table two feet square from the odd shaped board shown in the diagram. He did it in two sawings and wants to know if you can do the same.

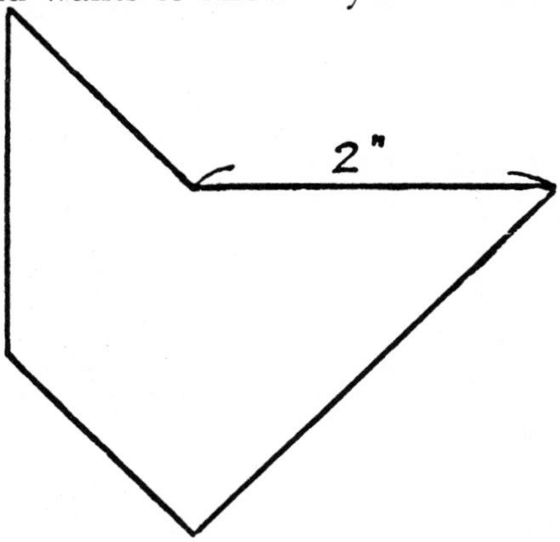

201. MY FAMILY AGAIN

The square root of the year in which my grandfather was born plus the square root of the year in which my son was born gives my grandfather's age when he died. In what year did Gramps die and how old was he?

202. STATISTICS

The sum of one-half, one-third, one-fourth and one-fifth the population of Wetfield is exactly the population of Ashkan. The sum of one-sixth, one-seventh, one-eighth and one-ninth the population of Wetfield is exactly the population of Garbij. What are the populations of these three towns, assuming that none of them is over 10,000?

203. SQUARING THE SQUARE

Transform the square shown below into five small equal squares whose total area shall be equal to this square.

204. IKE AND MIKE

Ike gave Mike as many dollars as Mike already had. Mike then gave Ike back as much as Ike had left. Ike, not to be outdone by Mike's generosity, gave Mike back as many dollars as Mike had left, which left poor Ike broke and gave Mike $80 altogether. How much did each man have in the beginning?

205. THE RULE MAY APPLY TO THE BAR

A uniform bar, thirty-one feet long, weighs one pound for every running foot. At what four points shall I cut this bar to give me four weights which will enable me to weigh, by combinations or single bars, every single pound from one to thirty-one inclusive?

206. SILVER THREADS AMONG THE GOLD

A man is the same age as his wife with the digits reversed. One-eleventh of the sum of their ages equals the difference in their ages. Assume the man to be the older. How old is the man and how old is his wife?

207. THE GREAT DIVIDE

Can you divide sixty-four into two parts so that if each of the two parts is divided by four and the two quotients are added, their sum will be one-fourth of the original sixty-four?

208. FAMILY FORTUNE

How can two fathers and two sons divide twenty-one one dollar bills evenly among them? Each must receive an equal number of dollar bills.

209. ACCURACY GAME

Give each player a pencil and some paper and, without referring to any of the objects mentioned, tell everyone to do the following:

1. Draw a circle the size of a quarter.
2. Draw a square the size of a postage stamp.
3. Draw a line the length of a standard cigarette.
4. Draw a line the length of a bobby-pin.
5. Draw an oblong the size of a standard playing card.
6. Draw a straight line 4½ inches long.

When the players have finished have them check their drawings with the actual objects to see how nearly accurate their diagrams are. The paper with the most accurate diagrams wins a prize.

210. ATOM BOMB

If A = 9 and G = 5 what is the sum of ATOM and BOMB or, in other words, what number does BINGO represent?

```
   A T O M
   B O M B
 ---------
 B I N G O
```

MYSTERIES AND DEDUCTIONS

211. THE RICHMAN ROBBERY

On the night of March 15th the New York home of J. Richman was robbed and $60,000 worth of jewelry was taken. The following five suspects were questioned and, from their statements, the robber was found and arrested. Knowing that each man made *only one* false statement and one of these five is the burglar, see how long it will take you to pick him out. This can be done only by using logic, reason, and good common sense. Obviously if a man says he is innocent in more than one statement he must be innocent since *only one statement can be false,* according to the rule of this problem. Par: 20 minutes.

Andy said: I was in Buffalo the night of the robbery. Butch is the guilty man. Charlie lied when he said the Dope did it. I am innocent.

Butch said: Andy lied when he said I did it. I am innocent. Charlie is not telling the truth about being in Buffalo. I never robbed anyone in my life.

Charlie said: The Dope did it because he told me so. I am not the guilty man. I was in Buffalo with Andy the night of the robbery. Butch is innocent.

The Dope said: Butch lied when he said Charlie is not telling the truth. I am innocent. Charlie is the man who did it. Ed was in Philadelphia on March 15th.

Ed said: I am absolutely innocent. Andy is innocent too. I was in Philadelphia on March 15th. Charlie was in Buffalo with Andy the night of the robbery.

212. THE BRIDGE OF SIGHS

Mr. and Mrs. Abrams, Mr. and Mrs. Banks, Mr. and Mrs. Cummings and Mr. and Mrs. Dennis all attended a two-table bridge party. No husband played opposite his wife and the Abrams' and Dennis' sat at different tables. Mr. Abrams played with his daughter who sat next to her husband. Mrs. Dennis played with her father who sat next to Mrs. Banks. Par: 10 minutes.

1. Who is Mrs. Abrams' son-in-law?
2. Who is Mrs. Banks' partner?
3. Who is Mrs. Cummings' partner?

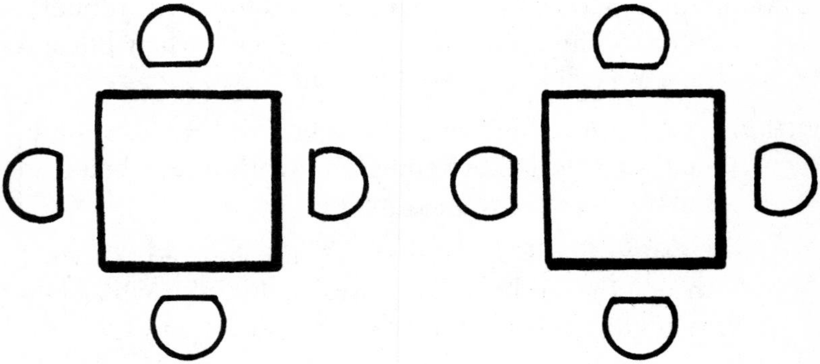

213. THE SECRET MESSAGE

In November 1944 a Nazi spy was caught in London and the following paper was found in his pocket. He claimed he was composing a song in praise of the British but Scotland Yard proved this to be false. What does the message really say? Par: 8 minutes.

Dear Walter:
Here is a suggestion for the theme of a song that I am composing for the British people. I take my hat off to them because they were the first to hold out even though they had no army or striking force to speak of. They never give up no matter what may come. It is useless to fight them further because our repeated attacks on them at Metz, Cologne or Aachen have been unsuccessful. They deserve great praise.

See you Friday night.
Hans.

214. FRED'S UNCLE

Six men sat down at a circular table to play poker. One of these men is Fred's uncle. Can you find him and fill in the diagram with the names of the other players from the following information:

Jim dealt the cards.
Tom sat opposite Fred and Joe sat opposite Fred's uncle.

The man who sat to the left of the man who sat next to the man who sat opposite Tom is Dick.
The man who sat next to the man who sat opposite Fred's uncle is Harry.
Harry also sat opposite the man who sat to the left of Fred.

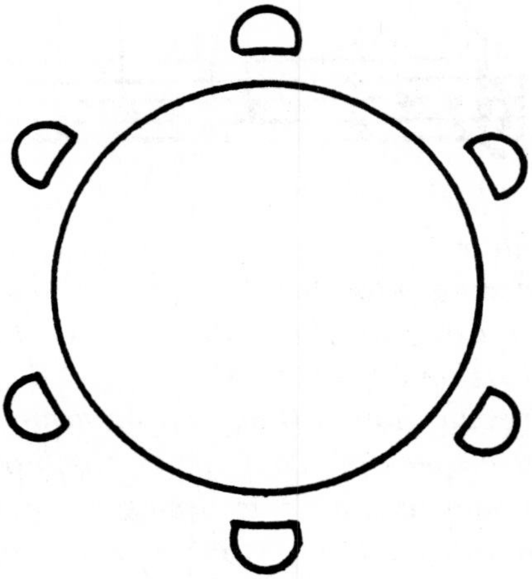

215. THE NINE PEARLS

Mr. Randolph bought his wife a Christmas present of nine real pearls, all exactly alike in appearance and size. The day after the purchase the jeweler who sold the pearls called Mr. Randolph and told him one of the pearls was a fake and could be detected because it weighed less than the others. Mr. Randolph tried to find the fake pearl by weighing each pearl but soon gave it up as a bad job. He took the nine pearls to the jeweler who located the lighter pearl in only *two* weighings. How did he do this?

216. SIX PATRIOTIC WOMEN

Six women sat down to dinner at a circular table as shown in the diagram. Can you identify each woman from the following information:

Miss A, who is not a Peace Corps member sat opposite the Army nurse.
Miss D sat opposite the WAC.
The WAVE sat at the Peace Corps member's left.
The Colonel's wife sat opposite Miss B.
Mrs. F sat at Miss A's right.
Miss D is not the nurse.
The Red Cross worker sat opposite Miss E.
Miss C is going to marry a marine.

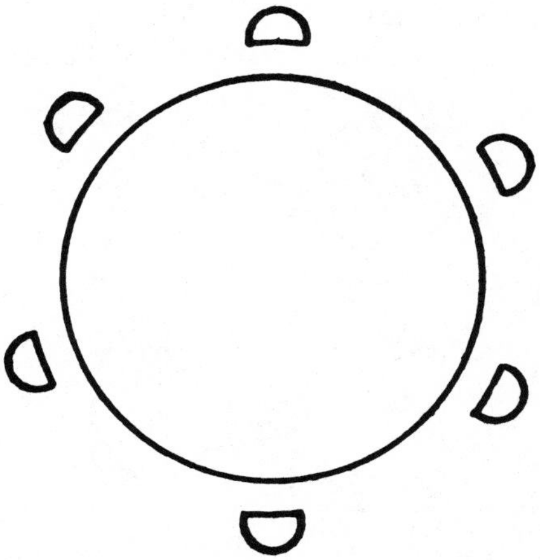

217. THE CLOCK MURDER

Josh Riggs, the young millionaire, was shot and killed one night by a burglar who fired two shots, one hittings Riggs and the other smashing the mantel clock into twelve pieces as shown below. The entire case depended upon the exact time that Riggs was shot because the suspected murderer proved that he was miles away between 7 and 9 o'clock on the night of the shooting.

It's up to you as a good citizen to see that justice is done to this man. In reconstructing this clock see that each piece fits into its neighbor like a jigsaw puzzle, and then print the hour in its correct place. For example: start with the piece marked 12 and try to find a piece that will fit into the right side of it. This will be the piece marked 1 as you can see. Do this for the rest of the pieces and you will have the time that Riggs was shot. Does the suspect go to the electric chair or not? Don't cut the pieces out, just put numbers in them as shown in 12 and 1.

218. THE COLLINS MURDER

At 12:22 A.M. on April 23rd, J. Morrison De Pew Collins, the millionaire banker, was murdered in his New York home. The following four suspects were questioned and their statements are given below. Knowing that each man made four statements, one of which is a lie, can you, by reason and logic, find the murderer? Remember, only one statement in each group is false.

Red said: "I am innocent. Shorty did it. I was in Florida the night of April 22nd. I never killed anybody."

The Rat said: "Shorty is innocent. Slim did it. I know nothing about the murder. Red was in New York the night of April 22nd."

Shorty said: "Slim is innocent. I am not the murderer. I was in California the night of the murder. The Rat was with me at that time."

Slim said: "The Rat is a liar if he said I killed Collins. I was in Philadelphia the evening of April 22nd. I never owned a revolver in my life. Red is telling the truth when he says he is innocent."

219. WHO IS THE CULPRIT?

Of eight suspects in a recent holdup, one and only one man is guilty. When the eight men were questioned they tried to mix up the police by admitting guilt and blaming the other fellow. Here are their statements. See if you can find the guilty man if we assume that exactly half of these men were telling the truth and the other half lied. After you have found out who the culprit is you can tell who told the truth and who lied. Here are the statements of the eight men: Time limit: 20 minutes.

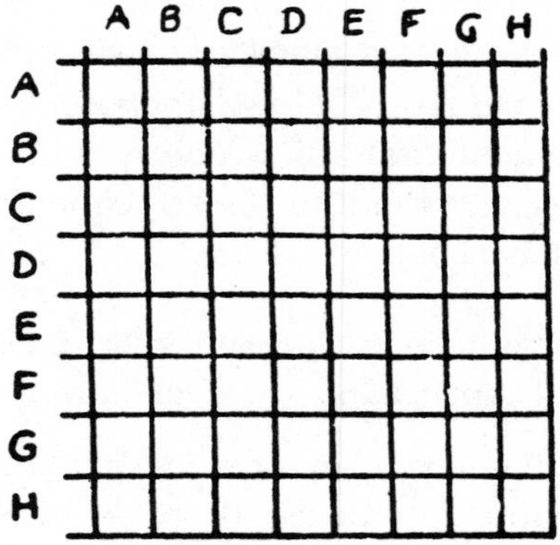

Cummings said: "Babbo is a liar."
Dillon said: "It was Flam who did it."
Abrams said: "I am the guilty man."
Higgins said: "Nobody did it."
Edwards said: "Flam is innocent."
Gunther said: "I am innocent."
Babbo said: "Gunther is the guilty man."
Flam said: "Gunther is a liar."

Hint: Use the diagram shown here and fill it in. Let a check (✓) be guilty and a dot (•) be innocent. Fill in each column, the letters representing one initial of the eight men.

220. THE F.B.I. GOES TO WORK

Three cargo vessels were sunk in 1944 between 40 and 200 miles east of Boston. The three sinkings occurred exactly a month apart. The F.B.I. caught the spy responsible and it was later shown that the following letter, found in his pocket, had a great deal to do with his conviction. Can you connect the letter with the sinkings and give the exact location and dates of each sinking? Here is the letter:

> Dear Eddie:
>
> My triplet sons are now in the Navy. The first SON gets $43.00 a month and saved $65.30 already. My second son gets $41.30 a month and has saved up $67.15. My third son gets $42.00 a month and has saved $68.00. All three entered the service on their birthdays, the 24th of March. They are all nice boys and I am proud of their thrift and patriotism.
>
> Yours
>
> Fred.

This puzzle requires considerable ingenuity. All clues are in the letter and, knowing the facts in the case, it is up to you to interpret the letter.

221. ALL PRESENT OR ACCOUNTED FOR

Seven U. S. Army Officers were standing in line, the highest ranking officer at the left. If no officer in the group is higher than a Colonel, can you identify them and fill in the diagram from the following information:
Grant ranks higher than Flory.
Adams ranks higher than Bradley and lower than Dobbs.
Carter, whose rank equals Evans, ranks lower than Dobbs and higher than Adams.
Flory ranks higher than either Evans or Dobbs.

○ ○ ○ ○ ○ ○ ○

222. MARRIAGE

Jane, Joan and Jean will marry the three men named below. Who will marry whom if:

> Peter is a lawyer.
> Joan is not engaged to the engineer.
> The doctor's future wife is not Jean.
> Mike is engaged to Jane.
> Arthur is the engineer.

223. MURDER WILL OUT

Three weeks ago five men were arguing about politics. One of the five shot and killed one of the group. Name the murderer from the following data:

Dave played five sets of tennis with one of the innocent men yesterday morning.

The murderer is Arthur's brother; they grew up together.

Edwin was interested in mathematics.

Charlie, who is a fine tennis player, used to be a bridge expert.

The murderer was operated on for appendicitis ten days ago.

Ben met Arthur for the first time only four weeks ago.

Arthur has been at his mother's ever since the crime.

Dave used to be a concert pianist.

Ben and Charlie played bridge together.

224. THE SPY

During the first week of World War II in Europe, when the Germans were closing in on Poland, a man was seized at Cracow and accused of being a spy. He said he was a census taker and had information on the population of Polish cities. In his pocket the police found the following note. What does this harmless list of cities with their population really mean?

City	1940 Population	City	1940 Population
Kratlact	684,371	Strawpnaw	583,149
Shronty	54,362	Dipeensef	1,498,675
Bieringo	437,586	Shawket	4,635

Why was the man arrested?

225. WHO IS GUILTY?

They finally caught the lone bandit who held up the armored truck and got away with $236,000. Using sound logic and careful reasoning, the brilliant District Attorney picked him from seven other suspects knowing that exactly half the suspects were telling lies but not knowing just who they were. See if you can do as well as the District Attorney.

Here are the eight men and what they said:

1. Frazetti: "Either Burns or Hoffman is guilty."
2. Adams: "I am the guilty man."
3. Cuminski: "Goldberg is telling the truth."
4. Hoffman: "Adams and Donovan are entirely innocent."
5. Edwards: "Let 'em all go; I'm the man who did it."
6. Burns: "I saw Hoffman do it."

7. Donovan: "Frazetti is innocent."
8. Goldberg: "Donovan lies when he says Frazetti is innocent."

Who is the guilty man and why?

Hint: Use the diagram and assume each man is telling the truth. Make a cross for "guilty" in each column. (The Frazetti column is done for you.)

	F	A	C	H	E	B	D	G
F								
A								
C								
H	X							
E								
B	X							
D								
G								

226. SECRET CODE

This simple little diagram was found in the pocket of a suspicious character in October, 1944. Can you decipher it and write out the message it conceals? Par: 10 minutes.

```
S. H E E O O
Y          A
N    13    R
Y          T
A          V
S U D C V L
```

227. FIVE RAILROAD EMPLOYEES

A brakeman, an engineer, a fireman, a porter and a conductor decided to have their pictures taken in front of a locomotive as shown in the diagram. Can you identify each man from the following facts? Par: 7 minutes.

The conductor is at one end of the picture.
The engineer is not Conway.
Brown is in the center between the brakeman and the porter.
Adams is the porter's cousin.
There is nobody at Edward's right.
Conway, who is nearest to the cab, lost to the conductor in gin rummy yesterday.
Adams stands at Edward's left.
Daniels' wife just had a baby.
Name each man in his correct job.

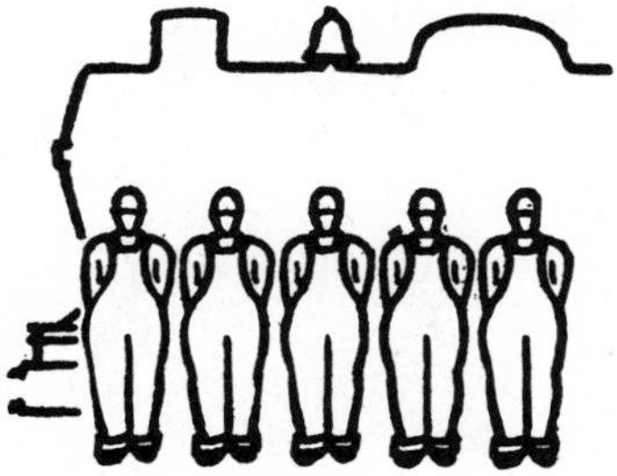

228. DOG LOGIC

Assuming that the following statements are true:

1. All dogs bark
2. Some dogs are terriers
3. All bulldogs bite
4. Some terriers bite
5. All terriers are dogs

Which of the following statements are true and which are false:

1. All terriers bark
2. Some terriers do not bite
3. Some dogs are not terriers
4. All barking dogs are bulldogs
5. All biting bulldogs bark
6. All barking terriers bite
7. Dogs that do not bite are not bulldogs
8. All barking bulldogs bite.

TRUE OR FALSE

The following sets of statements are either true or false. Some of them that seem to be obviously true are not and some that seem obviously false are true. On the other hand some that seem to be true are true and some that seem to be false are false. How many can you get correctly?

229.

1. The signal SOS means Save Our Ship.
2. Air is a very good conductor of heat.
3. Honolulu is the capital of the Philippines.
4. Every animal can make some kind of vocal sound.
5. A barrel filled with dimes is worth more than the same barrel filled with quarters.
6. The feminine for "Chairman" is "Chairlady."
7. Numismatics is the science of numbers.
8. An ellipse is the same curve as an oval.

9. Uranium has the highest specific gravity of all elements.
10. Every insect has six legs.

230.

1. All deer meat is venison.
2. Man-O-War won the Kentucky Derby many times.
3. A ladybird is any female bird.
4. A sandhog is a small animal that lives in the sand.
5. In a moon eclipse the moon is between the earth and sun.
6. Panama hats are made in Panama.
7. A Navy Captain ranks higher than an Army Major.
8. A titmouse is a small mouse-like animal.
9. Australia is the only continent entirely south of the Equator.
10. A steel marble will sink in any liquid.

231.

1. A water table is a table in a restaurant where water is kept.
2. A slide rule is used to add, subtract, multiply and divide.
3. A century plant blooms once in a century.
4. A firefly is not a fly.
5. Cats can not see in the dark.
6. Babe Ruth had the best batting average of all time.
7. The Star Spangled Banner became the National Anthem in Hoover's Administration.
8. New York City has the largest area of any city in the U. S.
9. There is more caffein in tea than there is in coffee.
10. Carding is another name for the filing of cards.

232.

1. The Bible says that Eve tempted Adam with an apple.
2. The new 200-inch telescope will be used to investigate the moon.
3. The bat is the only mammal that flies.
4. Mrs. is an abbreviation for missus.
5. A banshee is a kind of dog.
6. Meteorology is the study of meteors.
7. The letter "q" is always followed by the letter "u."
8. A mongoose is a species of wild goose.
9. The telephone plays a vital part in radio.
10. Calamity Jane was a real person.

233.

1. The Atlantic Coast is longer than the Pacific Coast.
2. The air we breathe is mostly oxygen.
3. Hyperbole is a mathematical figure.
4. Moonlight causes insanity.
5. Contortionists are double-jointed.
6. Dzugashvilli was one of the Big Three in World affairs.
7. It is possible to foretell definitely events in the distant future.
8. The sun always rises in the east.
9. St. Louis is the capital of Missouri.
10. All prime numbers are odd.

OBSERVATION PUZZLES

Every day we see the same objects over and over again. Day in and day out, week in and week out, we are always looking at certain standard things yet we fail to observe them. How many questions can you answer correctly about the one-dollar bill or the five-dollar bill or standard playing cards or the leading cigarette packages or your telephone dial? Here are five observation tests on these objects which will tell you how truly observant you are.

234. U. S. MONEY

1. Which way is Washington facing?
   a. to your right b. to your left c. neither
2. Which way is Lincoln facing on the five-dollar bill?
   a. to your right b. to your left c. neither
3. How many times does the figure 1 appear on the dollar bill?
   4 8 9 12 16
4. Where are the numbers of the bills located?
   a. upper right section
   b. upper left section
   c. lower right section
   d. lower left section
5. How many times does the word ONE appear on the dollar bill?
   4 8 9 10 11 12 16
6. What is pictured on the back of the five-dollar bill?
7. How many times does the word FIVE appear on the five-dollar bill?
   4 8 9 11 16 20

8. Whose signatures appear on these bills?
9. Does the great seal of the United States appear on either the one- or the five-dollar bill?

235. PLAYING CARDS

You Bridge and Gin Rummy fans, here is a real test of how well you observe the picture cards. Just write the correct suit after the number corresponding to the picture card. It's ten to one you don't get more than eight correct!

1. .... King
2. .... King
3. .... Jack
4. .... Jack
5. .... Queen
6. .... Queen
7. .... Queen
8. .... Jack
9. .... Queen
10. .... Jack
11. .... King
12. .... King

Note: Sometimes these pictures vary slightly but the cut of the hair on the Jacks and Kings and the position of the hands are always the same on all decks.

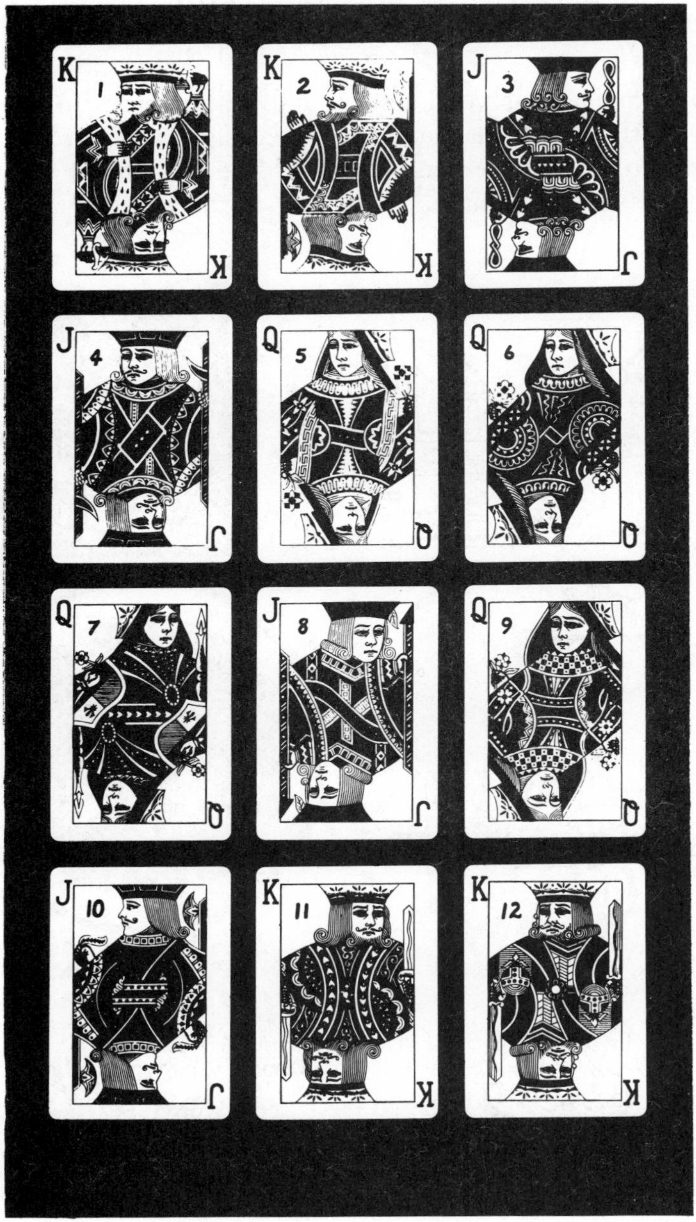
K 1
K 2
J 3
J 4
Q 5
Q 6
Q 7
J 8
Q 9
J 10
K 11
K 12

236. CIGARETTE SMOKERS

How quickly can you identify these six famous cigarettes? Only the design on the cigarette package is shown and if you are at all observant you should be able to get all six in less than a minute.

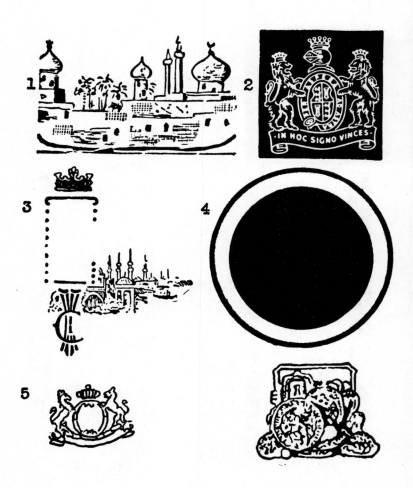

1

2

3
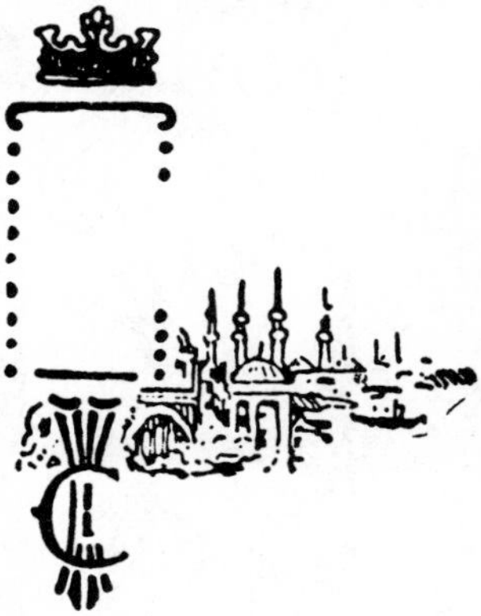

4

5

237. TELEPHONE DIAL

Everyone uses the telephone and most of us use dial phones. Can you fill in the correct letters and the numbers in this dial?

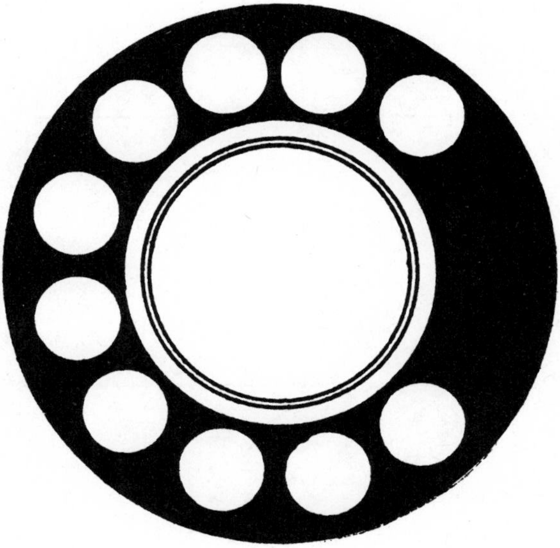

238. THE AMERICAN FLAG

It is amazing how few of us really know our flag. Despite the fact that we see it hundreds of times every day, only one percent of the people can draw the flag correctly from memory. We recently made a survey to check the truth of this statement. We asked one hundred people picked at random to draw the flag from memory. Only one man did it. He was a colonel and he had to make two attempts before he got it correct. How about YOU?

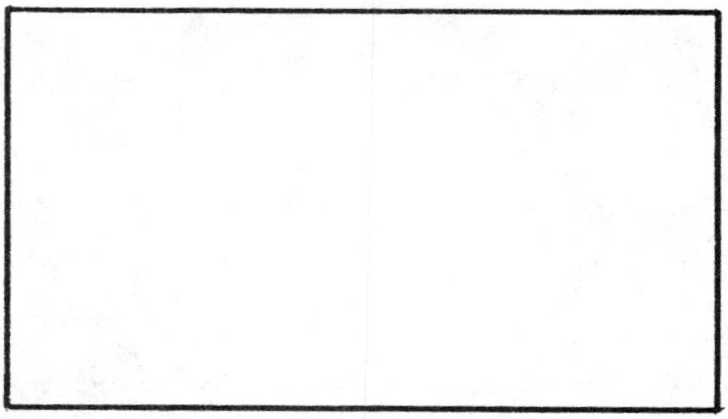

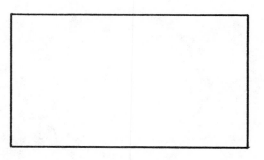

You can do this either as a solo or as a parlor game. If solo, just fill in the oblong to make an American flag and compare yours with an actual flag. If playing it as a game, give each player pencil and some paper and ask to have the flag drawn from memory. It's a pretty safe bet you won't get many correct flags.

ANSWERS

1. A FEW NEAT TRICKS:

a. Hold the card, rub your feet on the carpet or rug and slam the card against the wall. Static electricity will hold it there provided the weather is cold.
b. Use an ordinary soda straw and suck up the dime from one end.
c. Place them at right angles to each other and look into the place where they join.
d. Joe lit a cigarette, put some of the ashes in an ash tray, dipped the lump in the ashes and lit it. The ashes make the lump burn; without them it will not burn.

2. THE REMARKABLE EGG:

The story is impossible since peacocks don't lay eggs. The peacock is the male.

5. IF YOU DON'T KNOW, GUESS!:

1. The housefly would be as large as the moon.
2. 6.28 feet longer.
3. It would reach from the Earth to Mars and back three times!
4. It would make a pile of sand as high as Mount Washington and a mile in diameter at the base.

6. HOW GOOD ARE YOU IN PHYSICS?:

a. If the bird flies inside the cage the two together will weigh only four pounds because the flapping of the bird's wings pushing the air down will be driven out of the cage and displaced outside. If the bird were in a sealed box the box and bird would always weigh four pounds and three ounces.

b. The weight will go up.

7. WHAT ARE THESE TWO THINGS?:

The first is FIRE OR FLAME. It is neither solid, liquid or gas but merely a *process* of combustion. The second is your shadow which would be impossible to live without since sunlight is vital to us all.

8. A FEW "QUEERIES":

a. The proof of this amazing statement is simple. Cutting the paper in half 52 times merely means that you will have two raised to the fifty-second power sheets. The logarithm of 2 is .301 and 52 times this is 15.653. This is a number of 15 ciphers and turns out to be:

 4,503,599,627,370,496 sheets. There are about 450 sheets to an inch, so we have 10,000,000,000,000 inches for our pile. Divide this by 12 and you get a pile 834,000,000,000 feet high. Now, one million feet equals approximately 190 miles, so the pile would be 190 times 834,000 miles high. This comes out 158,460,000 miles.

 The pile of papers would therefore be 158,460,000 miles high!

b. Take a thin strip of paper and measure the distance on any geographical globe from Rio de Janeiro to Tijuana, Mexico (which is just below San Diego, California), and compare it with the distance from Rio de Janeiro to Cape Farewell, Greenland. You will find Tijuana further from Rio than Cape Farewell.

c. This is because gravity acts on both balls at the same time and no matter where the first ball is (provided it was shot horizontally) it will be 16 feet below the horizontal at the end of the first second, 64 feet below that horizontal at the end of the second second and so on. The same is true of the second ball which merely drops.

d. Water boils at 212° F. at atmospheric pressure. Decreasing the pressure lowers the boiling point, so if the water is placed in a jar and the pressure is reduced in that jar (air exhausted from it) the boiling point will gradually come down so low that it will meet the freezing point and the water will slowly freeze.
e. This seems odd until you consider that the size of one's shadow depends upon one's distance from the source of light. Since the sun is the source of light in this case and since it is 93,000,000 miles away, a difference of 450 feet in the two planes will make no measurable difference in the length of the shadows.

9. MUCH ADO ABOUT NOTHING:

Of course teacher is right. Multiplication is really successive addition. Five times a number is equivalent to adding that number five times. Zero is nothing and no matter how many times I add it I will still have nothing since I cannot make something out of nothing.

10. A LEGAL GEM:

C is entitled to the pearl according to most legal authorities.

11. WE PUT YOU ON THE SPACHT:

Photi is FISH. Ph as in Philadelphia, O as in women and TI as in nation.

12. THE $103 QUESTION:

A fifty, two twenties, a five and four twos.

13. GENTLE HINT:

14. THE ABSENT-MINDED PROFESSOR:

The time between a train *to* New York and one *from* New York is only two minutes. This leaves eight minutes between the departure of a train from New York and the arrival of a train going to New York. The old professor therefore had just four times as much chance of getting a train going to New York as he had of getting one going in the opposite direction.

17. PIGS AND PENS:

Just draw a large pen and then draw three small pens inside of it. Now put three pigs in each of the three pens and you will have an odd number of pigs in each of the four pens (the large pen has nine pigs).

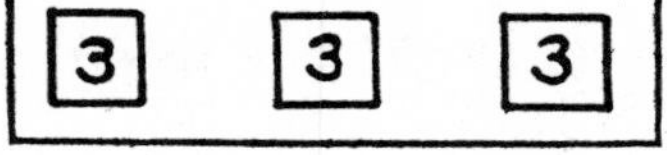

18. ODD MAN OUT:

Always start from the circle that is two away from the circle you started with previously. In other words you should put the next dot in the circle you previously started from.

19. A HOT ONE:

The sun.

23. CELLEMENTARY, WATSON!:

He ran the water in the basin and pulled the stopper up. In the Southern Hemisphere the water goes down the drain counterclockwise; in the Northern Hemisphere the direction is reversed.

25. DO YOU SPEAK ENGLISH?:

Here is the story translated into American:

"There was something the matter with our *car* the other day. After working over her for about *two weeks* I lifted her *hood* and found her *battery* was out of order. This necessitated my buying a new *monkey wrench* at the *hardware store*. It cost me *40¢*. Just at this point my *suspenders* broke, which embarrassed me because my *undershirt* kept showing. I suggested to my wife that we visit the nearest *department store* where she could purchase some *slacks*. She said this was a fine idea because she also needed some *pen points*, two *radio tubes*, an *electric heater* and a good *flashlight*, while I ought to get myself a new *hat*. After shopping we asked a *day laborer* to direct us to the nearest *lunch counter* where we could get some good *cold meat fried in potatoes and greens* and *warm soft-bread biscuits*. On the way home my wife expressed a desire to go to the *movies* but I preferred to sit in the *orchestra* of a good *vaudeville show* as there were too many *long lines* waiting at the *movies.*

26. THE CLEVELAND BUTCHER:

Pure logic for this one. C times CHOP must equal PORK. C can't be 1 since C times CHOP would then be CHOP and not PORK. C can't be 4 or more because C times CHOP would take up more than four decimal places, and PORK has only four places. Since we are told that C is greater than 2, it *must* be 3. We now have:

$$\frac{9\ .\ .\ 7}{3\ .\ .\ 9} = 3$$

Since P must be 9 and K must be 7 (3 times 9 equals 27). Now O cannot be 1, 2, 4, 5, or 6 as a substitution test will show. O must therefore be 8 and we have:

$$\frac{9\ 8\ 6\ 7}{3\ 2\ 8\ 9} = 3 \text{ which is correct.}$$

27. THE FACE IS FAMILIAR

$1	Washington
$2	Jefferson
$5	Lincoln
$10	Hamilton
$20	Jackson
$50	Grant
$100	Franklin
$500	McKinley
$1000	Cleveland
$5000	Madison
$10,000	Chase

28. THE MARK OF EVIL:

This is the signature of Adolf Hitler.

29. ITS IMPORTANCE CAN'T BE EXAGGERATED:

This is a map of the North Atlantic Ocean.

30. THE INNOCENT LETTER:

The words in capital letters give the message if you read them aloud:

SEA	OH	ENVY	OH	WHY	ESSAY	EYELESS	EIGHTY	OH	ANY	FRIDAY
C	O	NV	O	Y	SA	ILS	AT	O	NE	FRIDAY

31. ARE YOU WORTH YOUR SALT?:

Rub a comb briskly on your sleeve and bring it near the salt. Static electricity will do the rest.

32. IT HAPPENED ON THE GRAND JURY:

The receipt was folded after it was signed and the ink of the added items ran into the folds and showed tiny blots by the aid of a magnifying glass.

33. THAT MYSTERIOUS NUMBER:

The number is 1.

34. SEVEN ARCS AND WHAT THEY DO:

People merely dial a telephone number and get the party they want.

35. THE MOUNTAIN LAKE:

The chemist filled a ten-gallon tank with water from the lake and in it he dissolved ten pounds of concentrated red dye. After waiting a day or so for the dye to dissolve thoroughly he dumped the contents of the tank back into the lake. In two weeks he took another ten-gallon sample of the lake water and analyzed it for percentage of red dye. He found that it was one one hundredth of one percent, or one one hundred thousandth of one pound in the ten gallons. He correctly concluded that the ten pounds originally dissolved were distributed over a volume of 1,000,000 gallons which was about the number of gallons in the lake.

36. HOW COME?:

Jack and Jill are two of triplets.

37. FIVE STRIKES, YOU'RE OUT:

The words are: SMITE
MITES
ITEMS
TIMES
EMITS

39. THE MYSTERIOUS MAN:

The often-quoted, very mysterious man is the weather man.

40. WHITNEY'S MURDER:

Whitney must have been murdered between 2:10 and 3:00 A.M.

41. DOES IT MAKE SENSE?:

This, translated into everyday language, means that millions and millions are yawning and stretching, other millions are laughing loudly, and sneezing, and this is enough to make us all cry. This is foolish.

42. THE REMARKABLE BROTHERS:

Joe operates an elevator in the Empire State Building and Peter runs a bulldozer every day.

43. A HOT AND COLD QUESTION:

If you fill the cup with cold water it will not catch fire over a gas flame. The cold water will conduct the heat away.

44. THE ONLY WORD:

NOON

45. COLLEGE CAMPUS AND COURTSHIP:

Andrews-Notre Dame	Brown-Yale	Casey-Dartmouth
Dennis-Harvard	Evans-Brown	Fowler-Princeton

47. WHEN $4 = 8$:

The fallacy is in taking the square roots. There are *two* square roots of these two equations:

$$+4 - 6 \text{ and } -4 + 6$$
$$\text{and } +8 - 6 \text{ and } -8 + 6$$

Now $4 - 6 = -8 + 6$ and $-4 + 6 = +8 - 6$, so everything is safe.

48. SO BIG THE ARC:

The height of the arc would be more than 50 feet.

49. LOOKING INTO THE FUTURE:

The year is 1992. Divide it by 2 and get 996. Turn it upside down and get 966. Divide by 3 and get 322 and divide by two and get 161. Turn it upside down and get 191.

50. RED HATS AND GREEN HATS:

Everyone knew that the professor would not make it too easy for the boys and hence he must have hidden *both* green hats. If he did not hide the green hats, then any boy seeing two of them would naturally reason that he must be wearing a red hat. But suppose he only hid *one* green hat. Then Bill, seeing the other two boys with RED hats would reason that he either has a green hat or a red hat on. He would also reason that the other boys would reason the same way and hence say nothing since they would see a RED hat on him and another RED hat on the other fellow. Each would think his hat was either green or red on seeing red hats on the other two. Since both these boys hesitated in putting up their hands it follows that Bill must be wearing a RED hat just as the other two boys were and the professor hid the two green hats.

51. IT'S JUST ON THE SURFACE:

1. A ball or an egg or a football.
2. A cone.
3. A cylinder.
4. A triangular pyramid.
5. A square pyramid.
6. A cube.

54. TWO PAIRS OF WORDS:

WAVES to WIVES and SURF to TURF.

55. RAILROAD TRIP:

New York, New Jersey, Pennsylvania, West Virginia and Ohio.

58. AS EASY AS PIE:

The hostess cut the pie into four quarters, piled these on top of one another and made a single cut through the center making eight pieces.

59. COLD INDEED:

Twice as cold as zero has no meaning whatever, any more than ten times as cold as zero has. Any number times zero is zero. There is therefore no such thing as "twice as cold as zero."

60. TEN-WORD SQUARE:

S T A T E
H A V E N
A L E R T
V E R S E
E S T E R

This shows 10 different words for a top score of 100.

61. THE VANISHING BUILDING:

If B had left a forwarding address to his Miami residence he could well blame his housekeeper for not forwarding that important letter. Now, there is nothing in this story to show that B did this or that he even had a housekeeper, so it would seem that B is to blame for the neglect. On the other hand the building department should have sent that letter by registered mail, with return receipt requested—and there is no evidence they did that. In any case that letter would be returned to the department marked address unknown and it would not be for that department to try to locate B. It is clearly B's responsibility.

62. HERE'S A TOUGH ONE:

The only obvious way to describe the locations would be by road numbers all leading out of Polis. All these roads would meet in the center of this city and spread out just like the meridians. Each road would have to have a different number regardless of whether it continues over Polis and therefore goes in the opposite direction. Junkville might be described as South Route 14 while Coldberg might be indicated as South Route 7, etc.

63. THE AGE OF REASON:

This is really quite simple. The year of the California Gold Rush was 1849, and King Edward VIII abdicated in 1936. The square roots of these are 43 and 44 respectively. Grandpa is then 87 and the lad is 22.

64. A PROBLEM IN REVOLUTIONS:

The little wheel actually slides as it rotates and this sliding is so evenly distributed with the rotation that it is impossible to detect.

65. THE STRAIGHT-LINE CIRCLE:

This is shown in the diagram. Draw a square and divide the sides into a number of even parts as shown. Now connect A with A, B with B, C with C, D with D and so on until you have connected all the parts by straight lines. You can see that a quarter circle results. Repeat this process four times and you will have a circle made up entirely of straight lines.

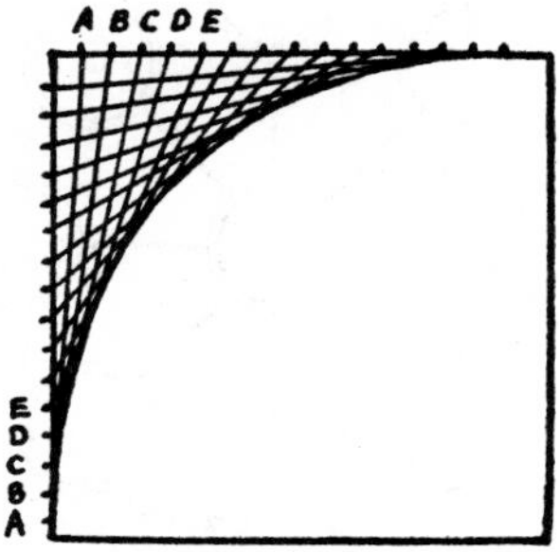

66. AND SPEAKING OF CIRCLES:

To get an accurate diameter tear off one corner of a sheet of paper and place it on the circle as shown. Where the sides of the sheet touch the circle in A and B, make two marks. Join these two marks and you will have a diameter. Half that line will be the center of your circle.

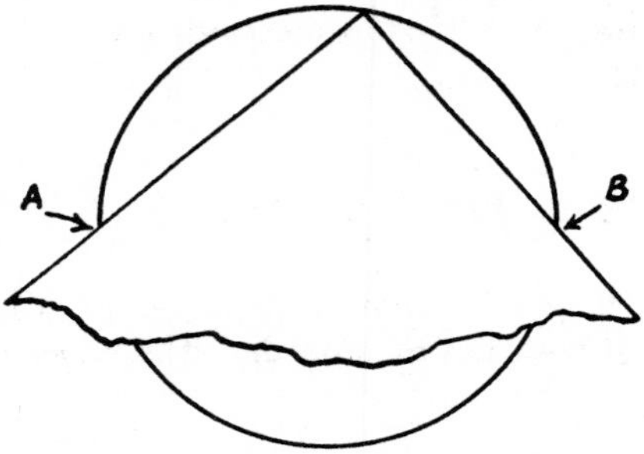

67. THE PUZZLE OF 30:

All you need do is put 10 in the center circle and the rest is very simple.

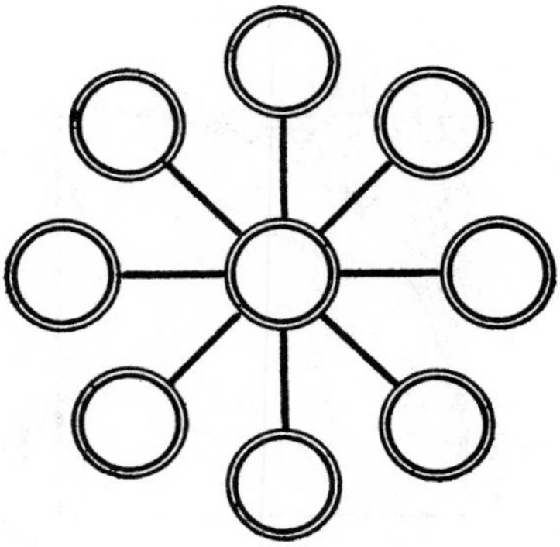

68. A NEAT TRICK:

The cup is tied to the doorknob with a bowknot. Cut one of the loops in the bow and the cup will not fall.

69. WHERE DID THE DOLLAR GO?:

The clerk gave back $5 and kept $25. The boy gave each man $1 and kept $2. Each man paid $9 *less* the $2 to the boy which makes the $25 given to the clerk.

70. THAT TROUBLESOME HYPHEN:

1. First-class 2. Attorney general 3. Fellow citizen 4. Boy prodigy 5. Four-fifths 6. Anti-American 7. Father-in-law 8. Semi-monthly 9. First aid 10. Lieutenant governor 11. Sky-high 12. Weather bureau

71. *CHERCHEZ LA FEMME:*

1. Spinster 2. Executrix 3. Author or authoress 4. Chairman or Madame chairman 5. Doe 6. Maharani 7. Baroness 8. Goose 9. Testatrix 10. Fiancée 11. Mare 12. Sow 13. Doe 14. Czarina 15. Vixen 16. Traitoress 17. Duck 18. Jenny 19. Abbess 20. Comedienne

72. OVERHEARD IN A PHONE BOOTH:

Here is the conversation corrected:
"Hello Fred. I feel *as though* I *should* call you up to tell you

that Edith and *I* are going to the beach next Sunday. Edith *said* to me the other day that she and the children want to get away and between you and *me* I think she needs the rest because she looks so *bad.* I told her that she is no different *from* anyone else. None of us *is* able to work through the summer without a vacation. Edith thinks I ought to join her and ask *whomever* I want to come along. I said it *doesn't* make *any* difference *whom* I ask *so* long as she is satisfied. I don't know *whether* you would like to come or whether I should ask one of my *brothers*-in-law, but, *regardless* of *who* accepts, I want you to be the first one invited by Edith and *me.* Well, old man, let me hear from you as *quickly* as you can because *if you can't come,* I was thinking *of asking* Peter."

75. THE MYSTERIOUS BATTLESHIP:

The man in the "crow's nest" traveled 105 feet farther than the others, due to the 100-foot increase in the radius of the earth.

76. A VULGAR FRACTION:

The fraction is 3/10.

77. A LIGHTLY PROBLEM:

Each bulb will cast a faint shadow on the wall.

78. FILLING THE WINDOW:

Yes, it will just fill the window. The sides of the second square equal the radius of the circle, or 17″, since they are diagonals of the four small squares. The radius of the circumscribed circle may be found as follows:

$$2x^2 = 17^2 \text{ or } 289. \qquad x^2 = 144\tfrac{1}{2} \text{ so } x = 12.02$$

This is also the side of the window, so a board 12″ square will just fit it.

79. I DON'T BELIEVE IT:

a. This is known as the "hydrostatic paradox." The pressure of the water on both bases A and B will be the same.
b. The smoke will go *down*. Try it and see.

80. HOMONYM QUIZ A:

1. Hoarse-horse 2. Taper-tapir 3. Be-bee 4. Bore-boar 5. Knew-gnu 6. You-ewe 7. Dough-doe 8. Flee-flea 9. Turn-tern 10. Bare-bear 11. Hair-hare 12. Ceil-seal 13. Mewl-mule 14. Links-lynx 15. Row-roe 16. Aunt-ant 17. Faun-fawn 18. Dear-deer 19. Earn-erne 20. Coarser-courser

81. HOMONYM QUIZ B:

1. Pare-pair 2. Cede-seed 3. Carat-carrot 4. Beat-beet 5. Leak-leek 6. Bury-berry 7. Flocks-phlox 8. Fur-fir 9. Been-bean 10. Plumb-plum 11. Currant-current 12. Beach-beech 13. Rows-rose 14. Time-thyme 15. Colonel-kernel 16. Charred-chard 17. Route-root 18. Tee-tea 19. Lief-leaf 20. Chute-shoot

82. A SUPERSTITIOUS QUIZ:

1. . . . going to kiss a fool 2. . . . cry before supper 3. . . . sit down and count up to ten 4. . . . someone is talking about you 5. . . . will get a letter 6. . . . you won't marry that year 7. . . . throw a pinch over your left shoulder 8. . . . knock on wood 9. . . . receive some money 10. . . . give him a penny 11. . . . a woman will call on you shortly 12. . . . pick it up 13. . . . make a wish

83. ONE AND ONLY QUIZ:

1. Franklin D. Roosevelt 2. Maine 3. Bat 4. Mercury 5. NOON 6. The sun 7. Buchanan 8. His fingerprints 9. Deny 10. 2 11. Rhode Island 12. Utah, Colorado, Arizona and New Mexico 13. 1 14. William Howard Taft 15. Panama Canal 16. Antarctica 17. "Are you awake?"

84. THE WORLD-FAMOUS PAT PENDING:

1-j 2-h 3-l 4-i 5-b 6-c 7-d 8-c 9-a 10-f 11-e 12-g 13-k

85. TRIPLET TIME TEST:

1-6-21 31-26-2 9-3-14 15-4-13 11-5-18 7-22-16 17-8-28 27-10-19 20-12-23 29-24-35 25-32-33 36-30-34

86. WHAT'S IN IT? TEST:

1. g o 2. p i 3. k 4. w c j 5. h a 6. b f s t 7. q 8. m

87. PAIRING CLICHÉS:

1-e 2-d 3-k 4-j 5-c 6-m 7-l 8-b 9-q 10-r 11-s 12-t 13-f 14-p 15-a 16-h 17-i 18-n 19-g 20-o

88. IT AIN'T NECESSARILY SO:

1. No. Astronomers can foretell eclipses with accuracy. 2. Not necessarily. If the cup contains dry coffee grounds it won't get wet. 3. Yes. 4. Yes. 5. Not necessarily. The main roof is only six floors high and you could jump into a pile of hay and not be killed. 6. No. 7. Yes. 8. No. Not in South America. 9. Not necessarily. 1900 was not a leap year.

89. HOW WELL DO YOU KNOW YOUR GADGETS?:

1 c 2 a 3 b 4 c 5 a 6 a 7 c 8 a 9 b 10 c 11 c 12 a 13 c 14 a 15 b 16 b

90. A GAME OF NAMES:

1-23 2-14 and 2-8 21-3 12-4 5-17 26-6 and 10-6 7-22 and 7-26 16-8 13-9 10-24 and 10-6 19-11 16-15 and 24-15 25-18 20-29 27-28 30-16

91. HOW'S YOUR ETIQUETTE?:

1-c 2-c 3-c 4-a 5-b 6-a 7-b 8-All except g and h 9-b 10-b 11-a 12-Mother should have Sr. after name.

92. WINING, DINING AND RHYMING:

1. café 2. clean 3. scare 4. beef 5. note 6. serve 7. bay 8. today 9. tang 10. stay

93. ARE YOU AN OBSERVANT SHOPPER?:

1. Planter's Peanuts 2. Campbell's Soup 3. Morton Salt 4. Underwood Sandwich Spread 5. Dr. Pepper 6. Ballantine Beer 7. Smith Brothers Cough Drops 8. Anheuser-Busch Beer 9. Maxwell House Coffee 10. Borden's Milk 11. Quaker Oats 12. Log Cabin Pancake Syrup 13. Sun-Maid Raisins 14. Sugar-Frosted Flakes

94. HOW GOOD IS YOUR MEMORY?:

1. bca 2. bac 3. cab 4. bac 5. cba 6. abc 7. bac 8. cab 9. acb 10. abc

95. LOW SCORE QUIZ (all *wrong* answers):

1. 64. 2. 1900. 3. The sun. 4. Nut. 5. El Paso. 6. Caesar. 7. Plant. 8. No. 9. In the Canal Zone. 10. Teddy Roosevelt. 11. San Bernardino. 12. Yes. 13. February 22, 1732. 14. Perscription 15. Yes. 16. Yes

96. CHARADE QUIZ:

1. Precise (press ice) 2. Castanet (cast a net) 3. Sausage (sauce edge) 4. Superimpose (soup primp pose) 5. Hibernate (high burn eight) 6. Ecstasy (X to C) 7. Annuity (a newer tea) 8. Nocturne (knock turn) 9. Restaurant (restore aunt) 10. Infirm (in firm) 11. Delicatessen (delicate SN) 12. Penitentiary (pen a ten sherry) 13. Largess (large S) 14. Metaphysician (met a physician) 15. Centennials (cent ten yells)

97. SLICED HAM QUIZ:

1. chisel 2. dismal 3. mashed 4. shield 5. malice 6. mailed 7. ladies 8. chased 9. chimes 10. cashed 11. claims 12. medals

98. THAT'S RIGHT, YOU'RE WRONG—1:

1. Yes. 2. Yes (Andorra). 3. No; it points to the North Magnetic Pole. 4. Yes. 5. 64. 6. Yes. Samuel Langley built the first airplane. 7. No; it refers to June 21 or thereabouts. 8. No; boric acid is good for the eyes. 9. Yes. 10. No.

99. WHO'S WHO:

1. Eye diseases 2. Maps 3. Talks shop 4. Gilbert and Sullivan operas 5. Tailoring 6. Children's diseases 7. Talks shop 8. Talks shop 9. Birds 10. Talks shop

100. JUST LOOK AROUND A BIT:

1. Very high 2. Up to you 3. Right arm 4. Up to you 5. To your right 6. King of Hearts 7. The Great Atlantic and Pacific Tea Company 8. Up to you 9. Right-hand page 10. Left

101. A REAL NOSY QUIZ:

1. Nosed out. 2. As plain as the nose on one's face. 3. On the nose. 4. Turn up one's nose or look down one's nose. 5. Under one's nose. 6. Bullnose. 7. To keep one's nose to the grindstone. 8. Nosegay. 9. Pay through the nose. 10. Count noses. 11. Follow one's nose. 12. Nosy. 13. Put his nose out of join. 14. Nose dive. 15. Put beans up one's nose.

102. UNITED STATES MAP QUIZ:

		3				4				3	
B.	4		2	C.	2		3	D.	4		2
		1				1				1	
		1				1				1	
E.	3		4	F.	3		4	G.	2		3
		2				2				4	
		2									
H.	3		1								
		4									

103. HOW WELL DO YOU MIX?:

1 c 2 b 3 a 4 a 5 c 6 a 7 c 8 c 9 a 10 b 11 a 12 b

104. GENERAL QUIZ:

1. INDICT 2. Ibis is a bird, ibex is a goat and ibid is a lizard 3. Strengths 4. Hannah 5. Powwow and glowworm 6. Havana 7. a 8. He shot one of them and they all died since they are all the same animal. 9. Mrs. 10. No; it will float on mercury. 11. A seal 12. Fur and fir

105. COLLECTOR'S ITEMS:

1 e 2 f 3 o 4 b 5 j 6 n 7 i 8 k 9 l
10 g 11 d 12 c 13 h 14 a 15 p 16 m

106. NICKNAMES, PAST AND PRESENT:

1. The Manassa Mauler 2. The Little Flower 3. Buffalo Bill 4. The Iron Man of Baseball 5. The Happy Warrior 6. The Brown Bomber 7. The Great Profile 8. Old Blood and Guts 9. America's Sweetheart 10. The Cowboy Philosopher 11. The Voice 12. The Wild Bull of the Pampas 13. Silent Cal 14. Lippy 15. The Tune Detective 16. The Kingfish 17. The Bambino 18. The Lone Eagle 19. Broadway Joe 20. The Schnozzola

107. WHAT'S IN A REAL NAME?:

1. Buffalo Bill 2. Mark Twain 3. Lewis Carroll 4. Mary Pickford 5. O. Henry 6. Marie Dressler 7. George Sand 8. Joseph Conrad 9. Tom Thumb 10. Irving Berlin

108. AN AMERIQUIZ:

1. Fifteen. 2. Thomas Jackson. 3. Iwo Jima. 4. . . . *when free men* shall stand between *their* loved homes . . . 5. The National Anthem, 4th verse. 6. F.D.R. was never a Vice-President as were all the others. 7. There are five rows of six stars and four rows of five stars. There is a row of six stars on top, then a row of five, then six, etc. 8. Honolulu, Hawaii. 9. Six. Columbus, Indianapolis, Denver, Boise, Cheyenne and Lincoln. 10. Breed's Hill.

109. TO BE SHOERE:

1. cold feet 2. cooling your heels 3. put your foot in it 4. on your toes 5. one foot in the grave 6. toe the mark 7. heel 8. the shoe is on the other foot 9. hate to be in your shoes 10. shake in your shoes 11. foot-loose 12. lick your boots 13. to boot 14. putting your best foot forward 15. stand on your own feet 16. started on a shoestring

110. LIST AND LEARN QUIZ:

1. Pyramids of Egypt 2. Walls and hanging gardens of Babylon 3. Temple of Diana at Ephesus 4. Statue of the Olympian Zeus by Phidias 5. Tomb of Mausolus 6. Pharos of Alexandria 7. Colossus of Rhodes
2. Superior, Huron, Michigan, Erie and Ontario.
3. Mercury, Venus, Earth, Mars, Jupiter, Saturn, Uranus, Neptune and Pluto.
4. Aries, Taurus, Gemini, Cancer, Leo, Virgo, Libra, Scorpio, Sagittarius, Capricornus, Aquarius and Pisces.
5. Alaska, Texas, California, Montana, New Mexico and Arizona.
6. Ringo Starr, John Lennon, Paul McCartney and George Harrison.
7. New York, Chicago, Los Angeles, Philadelphia, Detroit, Boston, San Francisco, Washington, D.C.
8. Gerald R. Ford, Richard M. Nixon, Lyndon B. Johnson, John F. Kennedy, Dwight D. Eisenhower, Harry S. Truman, Franklin Delano Roosevelt, Herbert Hoover, Calvin Coolidge, Warren Harding.
9. Venezuela, Colombia, Ecuador, Peru, Chile, Guyana, Brazil, Bolivia, Paraguay, Uruguay and Argentina.
10. John Adams, Thomas Jefferson, Martin Van Buren, John Tyler, Millard Fillmore, Andrew Johnson, Chester Arthur, Theodore Roosevelt, Calvin Coolidge, Harry Truman, Lyndon Johnson, Richard Nixon and Gerald Ford.

111. QUIZ OF THE MONTHS—A

1. From Janus, a Latin diety to whom the month was sacred. 2. January 30, 1933: Hitler came to power. 3. The evening of January 6, the feast of Epiphany. 4. February 2: the ground hog comes out of hiding. If he sees his shadow there will be six more weeks of winter. 5. Lincoln and Darwin: February 12, 1809. 6.

1847. 7. The sun crosses the equator and shines in the Northern Hemisphere. 8. From Mars, the god of war. 9. It is the first Sunday after the full moon on or next after the first day of spring. 10. From the Latin *aperire* meaning to open, referring to the budding of trees and plants. 11. It was started in Scotland to celebrate the coming of spring. It lasted from March 25 to April 1 and there was considerable gaiety and practical joking then. 12. "April, June and November . . ." etc. "Oh, to be in England now that April's there" "April showers bring May flowers" 13. It was started by John A. Logan, Commander-in-Chief of the G.A.R., on May 30, 1868 as a day for decorating the graves of the Union soldiers. 14. Maypoles came from branches of trees borne in triumph to the small town of Tudor in England. The branches later became poles. 15. Miss Anna Jarvis, of Philadelphia, who originated the first Mother's Day on May 10, 1908. It was officially adopted by act of Congress on May 9, 1914.

112. QUIZ OF THE MONTHS—B

1. D-Day. 2. The adoption of the Stars and Stripes as the flag of the United States, June 14, 1777. 3. The sun is over the Tropic of Cancer, or 23° 27′ north latitude. 4. Quintillis, or fifth month. 5. July 15. St. Swithin was buried near a cathedral where rain from the roof would always fall on his grave. On July 15 his body was removed from this place to a spot where rain was supposed to have been kept from falling on his grave. This angered the spirit of the saint, who decreed that if it rains on July 15 there will be rain for 40 days thereafter. 6. July 28, 1914: Austria declared war on Serbia to set off World War I. 7. July 4, 1776. 8. From the Emperor Augustus of Rome. 9. The Panama Canal opened August 15, 1914. 10. Japan surrendered, ending World War II. 11. The first atom bomb used in war was dropped on Hiroshima. 12. The first Monday in September. It was started by the Knights of Labor in New York City, in 1884. The first Labor Day was celebrated in Oregon in 1887 and this was taken up by other states. 13. The crossing of the equator by the sun, making equal day and night all over the earth. It differs from the vernal equinox because the sun dips into the Southern Hemisphere instead of the Northern. 14.

Septem, meaning seven, or seventh month. 15. England declared war on Hitler's Germany, September 3, 1939.

113. QUIZ OF THE MONTHS—C

1. October 9, celebrating the landing of Leif Ericson in North America, 1000 A.D. 2. October 31, the eve of All Saints' Day. It was the custom to drive away all evil spirits and spooks on this evening. 3. October 27. It was made official in 1922 and celebrated the birth of our navy on October 27, 1775. 4. No. It is the first Tuesday after the first Monday in November. 5. At 5 A.M. in a railway carriage in Compiègne forest on November 11, 1918. 6. and 7. In celebrating the fine crops in the first year of the Pilgrim landing Governor Bradford of the Pilgrim colony sent men into the woods to get wild fowl for a great feast. Turkeys were most prevalent and hence became the symbol of Thanksgiving. 8. *Novem,* meaning nine, or ninth month. 9. December 21; the sun is over the Tropic of Capricorn in the Southern Hemisphere. 10. From Christ's Mass or Christ's Church Festival. 11. Say St. Nicholas quickly and you will arrive at "Santi-Claus." 12. God's gift to the world (Christ) gave His life to save the world. These gifts in biblical times started the gift custom. 13. A record snow fell: 25.8 inches, beating the blizzard of 1888. 14. No.

114. ANIMAL SYMPHONY OPUS 1:

1. Meows, purrs 2. Barks, bays, howls 3. Whinnies, neighs, snorts 4. Hoots, screeches 5. Clucks, cackles 6. Grunts, squeals 7. Honks, squawks 8. Quacks, squawks 9. Howls, bays 10. Croaks 11. Baas, bleats 12. Barks 13. Gobbles 14. Hisses 15. Caws 16. Bellows 17. Coos 18. Roars 19. Brays 20. Chatters 21. Chirps 22. Peeps 23. Crows 24. Chatters 25. Laughs 26. Whimpers 27. Trumpets 28. Growls 29. Moos 30. Cronks

115. LIVING CREATURES QUIZ:

1. Wolf—keep the wolf from the door 2. Snake—a snake in the grass 3. Hog—road hog. 4. Cat—cat nap 5. Monkey—monkeyshines 6. Lion—a social lion 7. Ape 8. Cow—to cow a person into submission. 9. Fawn 10. Crow—to crow over some accomplishment 11. Whale—a whale of a good time 12. Bull—throw the bull 13. Horse—horseplay 14. Dog—dog Latin 15. Frog—a frog in one's throat 16. Lark 17. Seal 18. Chicken—chickenhearted

116. INTRODUCTORY VOCABULARY QUIZ:

1-7 2-6 3-2 4-8 5-1 6-3 7-20 8-9 9-11 10-10 11-13 12-17 13-14 14-12 15-15 16-19 17-4 18-18 19-5 20-16

117. VOCABULARY QUIZ—A

1-b 2-b 3-c 4-b 5-a 6-c 7-c 8-a 9-b 10-b 11-a 12-c 13-a 14-c 15-c

118. VOCABULARY QUIZ—B

1-c 2-b 3-b 4-c 5-b 6-a 7-b 8-b 9-c 10-a 11-b 12-a 13-c 14-b 15-c 16-c

119. UP-TO-THE-MINUTE ENGLISH:

1. Pertaining to television 2. German bombing plane 3. A conservative 4. A cylindrical rocket launcher 5. Machine for giving protons high velocities 6. Teen-age girl 7. A hired slugger 8. Swing music 9. A Jap suicide plane 10. A dilapidated auto 11. OK 12. Little people who make things go wrong 13. Portable two-way radio 14. Picked man to do very dangerous duty 15. A new man-made element 16. A war automobile 17. A traitor 18. A communist sympathizer 19. Situation Normal; All Fouled Up 20. Splitting of the atom 21. Part of a television set 22. British war plane 23. Sudden attack; also used in gin rummy 24. Term used in gin rummy 25. Supervised lodges for youths on hiking trips 26. A positive electron 27. A man-made element used in the atom bomb 28. A kind of vacuum tube 29. Multi-dimensional auditory perspective 30. A sheet of semi-transparent material which polarizes light 31. Legislator's grant of expense money 32. A Russian space satellite

120. TROUBLESOME PLURALS:

1. Daughters-in-law 2. Attorneys general 3. Brigadier generals 4. Judge advocates 5. Chargés d'affaires 6. Potatoes 7. Notaries public 8. Laws merchant 9. Opera 10. Pelves 11. Sergeants major 12. Teaspoonfuls 13. Piccolos 14. Tables d'hôte 15. Courts-martial 16. Paymasters general 17. Messrs. 18. Mesdames 19. Crises 20. Men-of-war 21. Lieutenant colonels 22. Banditti or bandits 23. Cannon 24. Phenomena 25. Aviatrixes 26. Menservants 27. Oboes 28. Oxen 29. Valets de chambre 30. Data

121. DUO-WORD TEST—A

1. MENACE 2. SEASON 3. OFFICE 4. ENDEAR 5. IMPAIR 6. COTTON 7. HATRED 8. ROTATE 9. BEGONE 10. DONKEY 11. PALACE 12. MARGIN 13. FOREGO 14. DAMPEN 15. SUNDRY 16. FARROW 17. WINTRY 18. ASHORE 19. CURFEW 20. ASPIRE

122. DUO-WORD TEST—B

1. CARPET 2. SEWAGE 3. CARROT 4. HAMLET 5. BIGAMY 6. PAWNED 7. ACTION 8. ADDLED 9. SETTEE 10. HERMIT 11. FINALE 12. TENDON 13. WARDEN 14. PUTRID 15. BARBED 16. FUNGUS 17. POTASH 18. LEGEND 19. SEETHE 20. ASSAIL

123. DUO-WORD TEST—C

1. DAMASK 2. SEXTON 3. RAGOUT 4. PUPPET 5. SATURN 6. BETRAY 7. TEETHE 8. METHOD 9. DONATE 10. BUDGET 11. ANTRUM 12. PARADE 13. SHEAVE 14. BUREAU 15. GOBLET 16. PIGEON 17. DOTAGE 18. MIDGET 19. RATHER 20. PALLID

124. DUO-WORD TEST—D

1. CAMPUS 2. TARTAN 3. LITANY 4. HEREON 5. LOTION 6. WINNOW 7. COMELY 8. CANADA 9. SUNKEN 10. BOTTOM

125. DUO-WORD TEST—E

1. CORNICE 2. EMULATE 3. PATRIOT 4. EARNEST 5. HISTORY 6. LEISURE 7. BRIGADE 8. SINKING 9. PAGEANT 10. KINDRED 11. RAMPART 12. HEATHEN 13. PARSNIP 14. CAPSIZE 15. HEARTEN 16. FORTUNE 17. DOESKIN 18. CAPRICE 19. IMPLORE 20. HEALTHY

126. DUO-WORD TEST—F

1. BARGAIN 2. ARCHIVES 3. BARRACKS 4. MUSTACHE 5. DISCOVER 6. TOGETHER 7. PENCHANT 8. BUTTRESS 9. HALLOWED 10. DENOUNCE 11. FARTHING 12. TOTALLY 13. MENTALLY 14. SPANKING 15. MODERATE 16. PASTORAL 17. MASSACRE 18. BRANDISH 19. FORESTER 20. IMPUNITY

127. DUO-WORD TEST—G

1. CANDIDATE 2. CABLEGRAM 3. CARPENTRY 4. PARALLELS 5. FATHERHOOD 6. PALPITATE 7. SEASONABLE 8. NOTICEABLE 9. FLAMBOYANT 10. PARSONAGE 11. ARCHITRAVE 12. ADORATION

128. FILL-IN PUZZLES:

a. ATE
TEA
EAT

b. TAP
APT
PAT

c. RAT
ART
TAR

d. TIME
ITEM
MITE
EMIT

e. SPAS
ASPS
PASS
SAPS

f. POST
STOP
TOPS
SPOT
POTS
OPTS

g. CARES
SCARE
RACES
SACRE
ACRES

h. RATES
STARE
ASTER
TEARS
TARES

i. TEAMS
TAMES
MATES
MEATS
STEAM

j. PRIEST
SPRITE
ESPRIT
RIPEST
TRIPES
STRIPE

k. MITERS
TIMERS

SMITER
REMITS
MERITS
MISTER

129.

B L I G H T
L O I T E R
M A S T E R
P O S T E R
M E T E O R
I N T E R N

130.

D A N G E R
H E A V E N
D O N O R S
C U R V E D
S T A G E S
S A U C E R

131.

V A U N T S
P I L O T S
P O O L E D
H E A L T H
S H A D E S
P L A N E T

132.

C L E A N S
D R I V E S
F L O A T S
M I N C E D
S T A T U E
L E A V E S

133.

C H A I R S
F L O O D S
G R A I N S
S P O R T S
S H I N E S
T A B L E T

134.

S P A W N S
C H A S E S
F I E N D S
H E A R T S
M E T E R S
S T O C K Y

135.

B O U N C E
C R A M P S
P A I N T S
R U D D E R
T H I N G S
S C R A P E

136.

H O T T E R
B E A R D S
C O A S T S
P I E R C E
S T A R T S
L E A V E S

137.

C L A M P S
P O I N T S
S A B L E S
S T E A M S
T R I P L E
C L O S E T

138.

N E A R L Y
P I R A T E
P I C K E R
S P I K E S
P L A N E S
S H O V E L

139.

M O T H E R
L O A T H E
D I N N E R
L A C K E R
S L O P E S
S T I N G Y

140.

B R A C E S
L A U N C H
P E D A L S
L O D G E S
S T A T E S
S I N G E R

141.

P L A C E S
B O A R D S
B I T T E R
M A N A G E
A S S E T S
R A N C H O

142.

C H A S T E
C H O R A L
C H I E F S
S O L V E D
S L A T E S
C A R E S S

143.

A R O U N D
S M E L L S
F E A S T S
P R I Z E D
S A L O O N
R A T I O N

144.

H A L T E R
S U P I N E
M E D A L S
R O O S T S
B A T H O S
N O R M A N

145.

J A R G O N
L E A D E N
S T R A I N
S H O O T S
H A R E M S
S T R I P E

146.

T H O R N S
S H I F T S
S T O O P S
T R A M P S
R E P E A L
S M A R T S

147.

E A S T E R
P S A L M S
M O T O R S
L A T H E R
P L A N E T
S H I N E R

148.

M A R R O W
G Y R A T E
H O R S E S
P O S T E D
S H I E L D
S E V E R E

149.

V A L L E Y
F I L I N G
S W O O P S
R U B L E S
H E R O I N
C A N T O N

150.

C L E V E R
S O W I N G
C A R V E S
P R I N C E
S N I P E S
S P I N E T

151.

C R A Y O N
T A I N T S
L A N C E D
F O R A G E
R I S E R S
S T E A D Y

152.

M A S K E D
L A Y I N G
T I G E R S
S T A P L E
S P I R I T
R E G A L E

153.

O L I V E S
P R E T T Y
C R E A M S
R E I G N S
P A T H O S
L E A V E N

154.

K N I G H T
P A L A T E
R A N G E S
W A I S T S
L I N E A R
N A V E L S

155.

J A N G L E
F E A S T S
G A R B L E
P A R S E D
S H A M E S
W H I S K Y

156.

C L I M B S
C R E A S E
H O A R S E
S A L V E S
M I D D A Y
M I D G E T

157.

G H O S T S
B R E A S T
G A U G E D
F I N D E R
B R I D G E
H U M A N E

158.

T A L L O W
E I T H E R
L I C K E D
D I C K E R
S T A R E S
T A B L E T

159.

1. P L A Y G R O U N D S
2. S Y M P A T H I Z E R
3. W O R K M A N S H I P
4. S W I T C H B O A R D
5. R E C O G N I Z A B L Y
6. S T E N O G R A P H I C
7. B A N K R U P T C I E S
8. S U B O R D I N A T E L Y
9. R E P U B L I C A N S
10. D U M B W A I T E R S

160.

1. V A L V E
2. G A U G E
3. T U B E S
4. T I R E S
5. D R I V E
6. L O C K S
7. S H A F T
8. M O T O R
9. S H I F T
10. F L O A T
11. P A N E L

161.

P L U M B
E X T R A
R E B E L
F L O R A
E L F I N
C O M I C
T A B L E

162.

F U N G I
O R G A N
U N D I D
R I F L E
T U L I P
H O U S E
O C E A N
F R A U D
J U I C E
U R B A N
L Y R I C
Y O U R E

163.

N I M B L E
O R D E A L
V A L I S E
E R O T I C
M A R K E T
B A N Z A I
E M B R Y O
R O T T E N

164.

C A L L O W
H Y A E N A
E N T E R S
R E L I S H
R A S H T I
Y E O M A N
T R Y I N G
R O C K E T
E S C U D O
E N S I G N

165.

F L O R A
L I T E R
O P T I C
A B A S H
T U T T I
A B E A M
T A S T E
I L I A D
O L I V E
N E S T S

166.

M O R A L
O U T D O
V I C E S
I N D I A
E A T E N
S L I N G
T A S T E
A V A I L
R I N S E
S O N G S

167.

G O B I
R A I N
A X L E
V I E W
I N S T
T R I O
Y A W N

168.

L O O M
D A D O
A M E N
V I S A
I D O L
N A Z I
C A P S
I D E A

169.

J U D G E D
E S T A T E
F A T H O M
F R E S C O
E X O T I C
R A N G E R
S A L I V A
O X Y L I C
N O B O D Y

170.

S E A G U L L
L A P I L L I
A S P I R I N
V E N A T I C
E M B A R G O
R O O M F U L
Y E G G M A N

171.

B E D L A M
E M B R Y O
E S C U D O
T Y M P A N
H O S T E L
O K A P I
V O T I N G
E I G H T H
N O U G A T

172.

S I L K S
A R E N A
L E V E L
T H E F T
S O L O S

173.

S E N D S
O V A T E
N A S A L
G R A I L
S L U M S

174.

E L I T E
L E V E R
U R E D O
D E L E D
E A G L E

175.

S O L O S
T H O R P
R O T O R
O U T D O
P O Y O U
S H O U T

176.

E L U D E
S K E I N
T E N E T
E A G L E
R E F E R
S H E D S

177.

C A T A M A R A N
B A N A N A S
N A S A L
B A T
F A T A L
C A R A V A N
M A H A R A J A H

178.

S L E E P S
H E A V E N
E D I B L E
E N D U R E
T E A R E R
S T E E R S

179.

G R A T I N G
R O T A T E D
S T R E E T S
T A N G E N T
S T E A L T H
E S T A T E S
G L U T I N G

180.

R E A D E R
I G U A N A
C A R R O T
H U R R A H
E N A B L E
R E N D E R

181.

S Q U A R E S
C H A R A D E
C A R A V A N
A L A B A M A
M A C A D A M
B L A T A N T
S T R A N D S

182.

S H U N T S
O U T I N G
U P T O W N
U R C H I N
F U M I N G
S O U N D S

183.

L I T E R A L
P L U R A L S
B R E W E R Y
E N C L O S E
P R E S E N T
B L A N D L Y
L A T E R A L

184.

M O D I C U M
A N I L I N E
B I S C U I T
I N S E C T I
C I R C U I T
S H I N I N G
M A X I M U M

185.

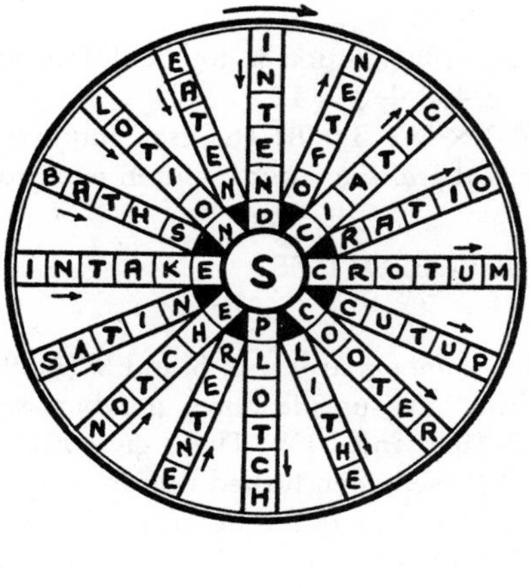

186. THE BARGAIN HUNTERS:

There must have been 7 women, each paying 29¢. There are no numbers, other than 7 and 29, that will make 203, and since the price of each article is more than 10¢, there must have been 7 women in the crowd.

187. FAMILY MATTERS:

Since my birthday is February 28 and NOT the 29th, I must have been born in 1900, the year divisible by 4 that is not a leap year. From this you can get my present age and my son's age.

188. FAIR AND SQUARE:

The word "among" means more than two people.

$$\text{Let } A + B + C = 12$$
$$\text{and } A \times B \times C = 9n$$

(there are 9 square feet in a square yard)

In this case the answer would be 4. But $4 \times 4 \times 4$ is 64 and 64 is NOT a multiple of 9.

Obviously the only solution is four children at $3.00 each.

$$3 + 3 + 3 + 3 = 12$$
$$3 \times 3 \times 3 \times 3 = 81 \text{ (81 is a multiple of 9)}$$

The answer is therefore: Four children each receiving $3.00.

189. MY YOUNG BROTHER:

Upside down numbers are 1, 6, 8 and 9 (omitting 0). The only usable 1900's that give upside down numbers when divided by 2 are 1922, 1932, 1936 and 1938. These give 961, 966, 968 and 969. The only one of these, when turned upside down and divided by 4, which gives a perfect square for an answer is 961. 961 upside down is 196, divided by 4 is 49, which is the square of 7. The year corresponding to 961 is 1922. My brother was therefore born in 1922 and he was 28 in 1950.

190. JANE AND PETER:

Use common sense for this one. My wife must have been born in the 1900's. There is only one possible solution. My son MUST be 12 because the cube of 12 is 1728. If he were 11 the year would be too ancient, 1331; if he were 13 the year would come out 2197. My daughter must be 14 which, when squared (196) and added to 1728, gives 1924. If she were 15 the year of my wife's birth would come out 1953, which is ridiculous, and it is hardly likely that my daughter would be 13 (which would make my wife's year of birth 1897). My wife was therefore born in 1924 and she was 48 in 1972. My age in 1972 was therefore 53.

191. TROUBLESOME FRACTION:

This is 2/5. Reduce this to tenths. We have, according to the problem:

$$8/10 + 2/10 \times 4/10 \text{ equals } 4/10$$

192. WHAT A GIRL:

This is not as bad as it seems. Dorothy was between 22 and 28. Her father was born in a year divisible by 8. The most reasonable years divisible by 8 for her father's birth are 1888, 1896, 1904 and 1912. Of these the year 1896 is the only one to fit the problem. This means that Dot's father is 50 in 1946 and she is 25. Now divide 1896 by 8 and you get 237. Add to this the square root of a certain Presidential year. There is only ONE Presidential year with a perfect square root and that is 1936. The square root of this is 44. Add 44 to 237 and get 281. Now the number of square inches in J Square feet is obviously 144 J. Dorothy's phone number was therefore:

$$237 + 44 + 144\text{ J} \quad \text{or} \quad 425\text{ J Eatontown.}$$

193. IT'S FUN TO BE FOLD:

The length of C-D is 9.23″.

194. THREE GENERATIONS:

Trial and error for this one. The year must be in the 1900's. Try 26 and 62. Multiplying these we get 1612 and certainly I was not married then. Now try 27 and 72. This gives 1944 when multiplied and is the only solution to the problem. I must be 54. Hence:

I am 54, my son is 27, and my father is 72.

195. THE JUNKVILLE RAILROAD:

34.6 miles.

196. PLEASE HELP ALICE:

```
    1 1 7
    3 0 7
    -----
    8 1 9
3 5 1
---------
3 5 9 1 9
```

197. SIMPLE GEOMETRY:

Large rectangle is 48 square inches. Small rectangle, 24 square inches.

198. HIGH FINANCE:

I had $7.50.

199. JAPAN'S LOSSES:

If S is 5, P is 4 and T is 3 we have to start with:

	.	.	4	5
	.	.	.	3
	.	.	.	8

By inspection N must be 9 and Q must be 1. We then have:

	9	.	4	5
	1	0	.	3
1	0	.	.	8

I cannot be anything but 2 and the problem is completed:

	9	2	4	5
	1	0	2	3
1	0	2	6	8

General Nuisance therefore took 10,268 prisoners.

200. THE CLEVER CARPENTER:

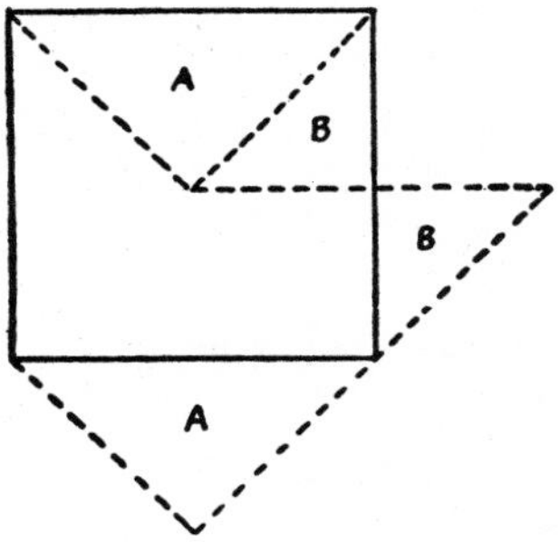

201. MY FAMILY AGAIN:

The only year with a perfect square root to fit my grandfather is 1849. This turns out to be 43. The next year with a perfect square root is 1936. This is 44. Gramps was therefore 87 when he died and he died in 1936.

202. STATISTICS:

The word "exactly" is important. Since you cannot have a fraction of a person it follows that the population of Wetfield must be exactly divisible by all numbers from 1 to 9 inclusive. The first number to meet this requirement is $144 \times 5 \times 7$ or 5040. Wetfield has a population of 5040 and you can go on from there.

Wetfield	5040
Ashkan	6468
Garbij	2750

203. SQUARING THE SQUARE:

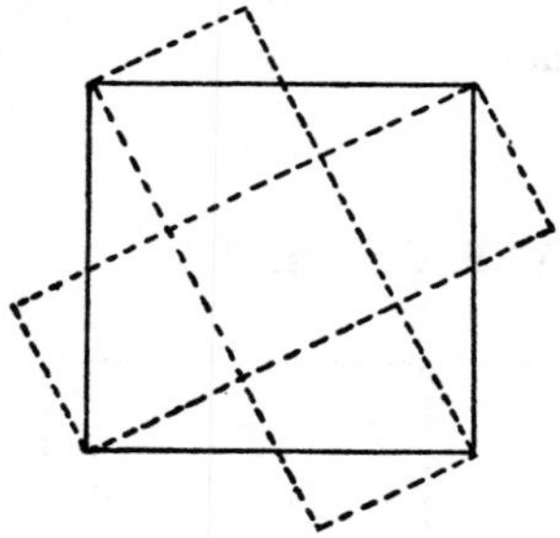

204. IKE AND MIKE:

Ike had \$50; Mike had \$30.

205. THE RULE MAY APPLY TO THE BAR:

Cut the bar at 1 ft., 3 ft., 7 ft. and 15 ft. marks, giving 5 bars of 1, 2, 4, 8, and 16 foot lengths.

206. SILVER THREADS AMONG THE GOLD:

Man is 54, wife is 45. Sum is 99, difference is 9.

207. THE GREAT DIVIDE:

The two parts are 40 and 24. $10 + 6$ is 16.

208. FAMILY FORTUNE:

A grandfather, a father and a son divided the 21 bills so that each got $7.00. There were still two fathers and two sons in the group.

210. ATOM BOMB:

B must be equal to 1 and 1 is therefore 0. We then have:

$$\begin{array}{rrrrr} & 9 & \cdot & \cdot & \cdot \\ & 1 & \cdot & \cdot & 1 \\ \hline 1 & 0 & \cdot & 5 & \cdot \end{array}$$

From this it follows that $M = 2$ and $O = 3$. We then have:

$$\begin{array}{rrrrr} & 9 & 4 & 3 & 2 \\ & 1 & 3 & 2 & 1 \\ \hline 1 & 0 & 7 & 5 & 3 \end{array}$$

211. THE RICHMAN ROBBERY:

Ed is the robber. If Andy were in Buffalo the night of the robbery he must be innocent. If this is true and "I am innocent" is true he is surely innocent. Now go to Butch. He says "I'm innocent" and "I never robbed anyone in my life." Butch MUST be innocent according to rule. "Butch is the guilty man" is Andy's only false statement. Butch's only false statement is therefore "Charlie is not telling the truth about being in Buffalo." Since this is false it follows that Charlie's only false statement is "The dope did it, etc." Since the Dope is obviously innocent, Ed must be guilty.

212. THE BRIDGE OF SIGHS:

1. Mr. Cummings 2. Mr. Dennis 3. Mr. Abrams

213. THE SECRET MESSAGE:

The notes give the clue. They are B F A A A A F.

The first word beginning with B is *British.* The first word after British beginning with F is *first.* The first word after *first* beginning with A is *army* and so on. The message is:

BRITISH FIRST ARMY ATTACKS AT AACHEN FRIDAY.

214. FRED'S UNCLE:

JOE

HARRY FRED

TOM JIM

DICK (FRED'S UNCLE)

215. THE NINE PEARLS:

The jeweler divided the nine pearls into three groups of three each. He then weighed three against three. If they just balanced the light pearl was not amongst them and must be in the remaining three. If they did not balance the light pearl was among the lighter three. In either case he knows that the light pearl is among three instead of nine. He now weighs two of the remaining three. If the scales balance the one left over is the fake pearl; if they do not balance; he can locate the lighter pearl on the scales.

216. SIX PATRIOTIC WOMEN:

Note that the Colonel's wife is the only Mrs. She must therefore be Mrs. F. Now Miss B is obviously not the Colonel's wife. She is not the nurse and she is not the Red Cross worker. She must be the WAVE or the Peace Corps member. By working with the diagram and using logic you will find that:

Miss A is the Red Cross worker, Miss B is the WAVE, Miss C is the WAC, Miss D is the Peace Corps member, Miss E is the nurse and Mrs. F is the Colonel's wife.

217. THE CLOCK MURDER:

Now, start with the piece marked 1 and look for the piece that fits into the right side of 1. This is just below it to the right. Call this 2. Now do the same for piece 2 and keep on until you have every hour numbered. You will see that the hour hand points to 8 and the minute hand is 4 minutes before 12. The time is therefore 7:56 and the suspect was miles away at that time. He is therefore innocent.

218. THE COLLINS MURDER:

Slim is guilty. Red must be innocent since two of his statements say so and they cannot both be false. His other two statements are "Shorty did it" and "I was in Florida the night of April 22." Now Shorty is clearly innocent because two of his statements say he is not the murderer. This makes "Shorty did it" Red's only false statement and the statement about being in Florida is therefore true. Now look at the Rat's statements. Obviously the only false statement here is "Red was in New York the night of April 22." This makes the statement "Slim did it" a true one.

219. "WHO IS THE CULPRIT?"

Abrams is the guilty man. The diagram should be filled out as follows, using a check for guilty and a dot for innocent:

You can see that the only row containing 4 dots and 4 checks is the A row. Hence Abrams is the culprit and you can tell which of the others told the truth and which lied.

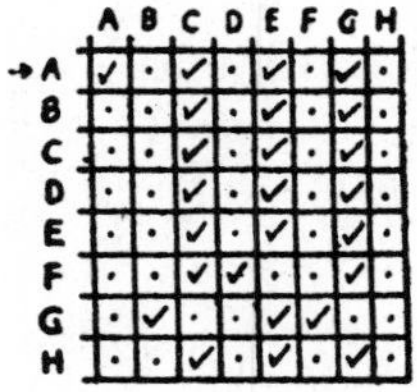

220. THE F.B.I. GOES TO WORK:

We know the ships were sunk a month apart . . . and in the fall. The capitalizing of the word SON suggests the three fall months in that order: September, October and November and the birthday date of the 24th gives us the three dates of the sinkings. Since the sinkings took place off Boston we can see right away that the salaries and savings fit the latitude and longitude. We then have:

Vessel 1 sunk Sept. 24 at Lat 43°, Long 65° 30′ W.
Vessel 2 sunk Oct. 24 at Lat 41° 30′ N., Long 67° 15′ W.
Vessel 3 sunk Nov. 24 at Lat 42° N., Long 68° W.

221. ALL PRESENT OR ACCOUNTED FOR:

Grant	Flory	Dobbs
O	O	O
Colonel	Lt. Colonel	Major
Carter and Evans	Adams	Bradley
O O	O	O
Captains	1st Lieut.	2nd Lieut.

222. MARRIAGE:

Jane will marry Mike. Jean will marry Arthur. Joan will marry Peter.

223. MURDER WILL OUT:

Charlie killed Edwin!

Dave can't be the murderer for he played five sets of tennis and the murderer was operated on ten days ago.

Arthur is not the murderer but the murderer's brother.

Ben is not the murderer for he met Arthur, for the first time, four weeks ago.

This leaves Charlie and Edwin. Since Charlie is obviously alive (he is a fine tennis player) he must have killed Edwin, the only other name mentioned.

224. THE SPY:

The "populations" give the number of the letters in the words, thus: Strawpnaw — 583,149 means the 5th, the 8th, the 3rd, the 1st, the 4th, and the 9th letters in this word. This spells Warsaw. Doing the same for the other five words, we get:

ATTACK NORTH REGION
WARSAW DEFENSE WEAK

225. WHO IS GUILTY?:

Hoffman is the guilty man.

When you have filled out the diagram as shown below you will have one row which contains four crosses — the only row that does. This indicates four true and four false, which answers the requirements of the problem. The H row is Hoffman and you can easily check this result in the problem.

	F	A	C	H	E	B	D	G	
F			X	X				X	
A		X					X		
C				X			X		
H	X			X		X	X		◆
E				X	X		X		
B	X			X			X		
D							X		
G				X			X		

226. SECRET CODE:

By starting at S (with the dot) and counting every thirteenth letter, we get:

CONVOY LEAVES THURSDAY

227. FIVE RAILROAD EMPLOYEES:

Edwards—conductor
Adams—brakeman
Brown—engineer
Daniels—porter
Conway—fireman

228. DOG LOGIC:

1, 2, 3, 5, 7 and 8 are true.

229. 1. False. SOS is a code signal, adopted because it is easy to transmit and distinguish. There is no phrase for which the letters stand. 2. False. It is a very poor conductor. 3. False. Manila is. 4. False. A giraffe cannot make any vocal sound. 5. True. 6. False. It is Chairman. 7. False. It is the study of coins. 8. False. It is popularly known as oval but mathematically it is entirely different. 9. False. Osmium has the highest specific gravity of all elements. 10. True.

230. 1. True. 2. False. 3. False. It is a bug. 4. False. A sand hog is a man who digs tunnels under rivers. 5. False. 6. False. They are made in Ecuador. 7. True. 8. False. It is a bird. 9. False. Antarctica is another. 10. False. It will float on mercury.

231. 1. False. It is a projecting ledge of masonry on the side of a building. 2. False. A slide rule does not add or subtract. 3. True. It blooms once and dies. 4. True. It is a beetle. 5. True. 6. False. Hugh Duffy of Boston was the all time batting champ—average .434. 7. True. 8. False. Los Angeles has. 9. True. Tea contains 2% to 5%; coffee from .8% to 1.7%. 10. False.

232. 1. False. The Bible makes no mention of an apple. 2. False. It is too big for such close observation. 3. True. 4. False. It is the abbreviation for mistress. 5. False. 6. False. It is the study

of weather. 7. False. In "Iraqis" it is not. 8. False. It is a small mammal. 9. True. 10. Her name was Martha Jane Burke, born in 1852.

233. 1. True. 2. False. It is about 80% nitrogen. 3. False. 4. False. 5. False. 6. True. He is Joseph Stalin. 7. True. Eclipses of the sun and moon may be foretold with certainty. 8. False. Most times it rises in the southeast or northeast. 9. False. 10. False. 2 is a prime number.

234. U. S. MONEY:

1.a 2.a 3.8 4.a and d 5.8 6. The Lincoln Memorial 7.11 8. The Treasurer of the United States and The Secretary of the Treasury 9. Yes

235. PLAYING CARDS:

1. Heart 2. Diamond 3. Spade 4. Diamond 5. Heart 6. Club 7. Spade 8. Club 9. Diamond 10. Heart 11. Spade 12. Club

236. CIGARETTE SMOKERS:

1. Camel 2. Pall Mall 3. Chesterfields 4. Lucky Strikes 5. Philip Morris 6. Old Gold

237. TELEPHONE DIAL:

First hole	— 1			
2nd	"	— ABC . .	and	2
3rd	"	— DEF . .	"	3
4th	"	— GHI . .	"	4
5th	"	— JKL . . .	"	5
6th	"	— MNO . .	"	6
7th	"	— PRS . .	"	7
8th	"	— TUV . .	"	8
9th	"	— WXY . .	"	9
10th	"	— Operator	"	0

238.

A CATALOG OF SELECTED

DOVER BOOKS

IN ALL FIELDS OF INTEREST

A CATALOG OF SELECTED DOVER BOOKS IN ALL FIELDS OF INTEREST

TOLL HOUSE TRIED AND TRUE RECIPES, Ruth Graves Wakefield. Popovers, veal and ham loaf, baked beans, much more from the famous Mass. restaurant. Nearly 700 recipes. 376pp. 5⅜ × 8½. 23560-2 Pa. $4.95

FAVORITE CHRISTMAS CAROLS, selected and arranged by Charles J.F. Cofone. Title, music, first verse and refrain of 34 traditional carols in handsome calligraphy; also subsequent verses and other information in type. 79pp. 8⅜ × 11. 20445-6 Pa. $3.50

CAMERA WORK: A PICTORIAL GUIDE, Alfred Stieglitz. All 559 illustrations from most important periodical in history of art photography. Reduced in size but still clear, in strict chronological order, with complete captions. 176pp. 8⅜ × 11¼. 23591-2 Pa. $6.95

FAVORITE SONGS OF THE NINETIES, edited by Robert Fremont. 88 favorites: "Ta-Ra-Ra-Boom-De-Aye," "The Band Played On," "Bird in a Gilded Cage," etc. 401pp. 9 × 12. 21536-9 Pa. $12.95

STRING FIGURES AND HOW TO MAKE THEM, Caroline F. Jayne. Fullest, clearest instructions on string figures from around world: Eskimo, Navajo, Lapp, Europe, more. Cat's cradle, moving spear, lightning, stars. 950 illustrations. 407pp. 5⅜ × 8½. 20152-X Pa. $5.95

LIFE IN ANCIENT EGYPT, Adolf Erman. Detailed older account, with much not in more recent books: domestic life, religion, magic, medicine, commerce, and whatever else needed for complete picture. Many illustrations. 597pp. 5⅜ × 8½. 22632-8 Pa. $7.95

ANCIENT EGYPT: ITS CULTURE AND HISTORY, J.E. Manchip White. From pre-dynastics through Ptolemies: scoiety, history, political structure, religion, daily life, literature, cultural heritage. 48 plates. 217pp. 5⅜ × 8½. (EBE) 22548-8 Pa. $4.95

KEPT IN THE DARK, Anthony Trollope. Unusual short novel about Victorian morality and abnormal psychology by the great English author. Probably the first American publication. Frontispiece by Sir John Millais. 92pp. 6½ × 9¼. 23609-9 Pa. $2.95

MAN AND WIFE, Wilkie Collins. Nineteenth-century master launches an attack on out-moded Scottish marital laws and Victorian cult of athleticism. Artfully plotted. 35 illustrations. 239pp. 6⅛ × 9¼. 24451-2 Pa. $5.95

RELATIVITY AND COMMON SENSE, Herman Bondi. Radically reoriented presentation of Einstein's Special Theory and one of most valuable popular accounts available. 60 illustrations. 177pp. 5⅜ × 8. (EUK) 24021-5 Pa. $3.95

THE EGYPTIAN BOOK OF THE DEAD, E.A. Wallis Budge. Complete reproduction of Ani's papyrus, finest ever found. Full hieroglyphic text, interlinear transliteration, word-for-word translation, smooth translation. 533pp. 6½ × 9¼. (USO) 21866-X Pa. $8.95

COUNTRY AND SUBURBAN HOMES OF THE PRAIRIE SCHOOL PERIOD, H.V. von Holst. Over 400 photographs floor plans, elevations, detailed drawings (exteriors and interiors) for over 100 structures. Text. Important primary source. 128pp. 8⅜ × 11¼. 24373-7 Pa. $5.95

YUCATAN BEFORE AND AFTER THE CONQUEST, Diego de Landa. Only significant account of Yucatan written in the early post-Conquest era. Translated by William Gates. Over 120 illustrations. 162pp. 5⅜ × 8½. 23622-6 Pa. $3.50

ORNATE PICTORIAL CALLIGRAPHY, E.A. Lupfer. Complete instructions, over 150 examples help you create magnificent "flourishes" from which beautiful animals and objects gracefully emerge. 8⅛ × 11. 21957-7 Pa. $2.95

DOLLY DINGLE PAPER DOLLS, Grace Drayton. Cute chubby children by same artist who did Campbell Kids. Rare plates from 1910s. 30 paper dolls and over 100 outfits reproduced in full color. 32pp. 9¼ × 12¼. 23711-7 Pa. $3.50

CURIOUS GEORGE PAPER DOLLS IN FULL COLOR, H. A. Rey, Kathy Allert. Naughty little monkey-hero of children's books in two doll figures, plus 48 full-color costumes: pirate, Indian chief, fireman, more. 32pp. 9¼ × 12¼. 24386-9 Pa. $3.50

GERMAN: HOW TO SPEAK AND WRITE IT, Joseph Rosenberg. Like *French, How to Speak and Write It.* Very rich modern course, with a wealth of pictorial material. 330 illustrations. 384pp. 5⅜ × 8½. (USUKO) 20271-2 Pa. $4.75

CATS AND KITTENS: 24 Ready-to-Mail Color Photo Postcards, D. Holby. Handsome collection; feline in a variety of adorable poses. Identifications. 12pp. on postcard stock. 8¼ × 11. 24469-5 Pa. $2.95

MARILYN MONROE PAPER DOLLS, Tom Tierney. 31 full-color designs on heavy stock, from *The Asphalt Jungle, Gentlemen Prefer Blondes,* 22 others. 1 doll. 16 plates. 32pp. 9⅜ × 12¼. 23769-9 Pa. $3.50

FUNDAMENTALS OF LAYOUT, F.H. Wills. All phases of layout design discussed and illustrated in 121 illustrations. Indispensable as student's text or handbook for professional. 124pp. 8⅜ × 11. 21279-3 Pa. $4.50

FANTASTIC SUPER STICKERS, Ed Sibbett, Jr. 75 colorful pressure-sensitive stickers. Peel off and place for a touch of pizzazz: clowns, penguins, teddy bears, etc. Full color. 16pp. 8¼ × 11. 24471-7 Pa. $2.95

LABELS FOR ALL OCCASIONS, Ed Sibbett, Jr. 6 labels each of 16 different designs—baroque, art nouveau, art deco, Pennsylvania Dutch, etc.—in full color. 24pp. 8¼ × 11. 23688-9 Pa. $2.95

HOW TO CALCULATE QUICKLY: RAPID METHODS IN BASIC MATHEMATICS, Henry Sticker. Addition, subtraction, multiplication, division, checks, etc. More than 8000 problems, solutions. 185pp. 5 × 7¼. 20295-X Pa. $2.95

THE CAT COLORING BOOK, Karen Baldauski. Handsome, realistic renderings of 40 splendid felines, from American shorthair to exotic types. 44 plates. Captions. 48pp. 8¼ × 11. 24011-8 Pa. $2.25

THE TALE OF PETER RABBIT, Beatrix Potter. The inimitable Peter's terrifying adventure in Mr. McGregor's garden, with all 27 wonderful, full-color Potter illustrations. 55pp. 4¼ × 5½. (Available in U.S. only) 22827-4 Pa. $1.75

BASIC ELECTRICITY, U.S. Bureau of Naval Personnel. Batteries, circuits, conductors, AC and DC, inductance and capacitance, generators, motors, transformers, amplifiers, etc. 349 illustrations. 448pp. 6½ × 9¼. 20973-3 Pa. $7.95